THE PUBLIC SIDE OF LEARNING

American Academy of Religion
Studies in Religion

Editors
Charley Hardwick
James O. Duke

Number 40

THE PUBLIC SIDE OF LEARNING
The Political Consequences of Scholarship
in the Context of Judaism
by
Jacob Neusner

THE PUBLIC SIDE
OF LEARNING

The Political Consequences of Scholarship
in the Context of Judaism

JACOB NEUSNER

Scholars Press
Chico, California

THE PUBLIC SIDE OF LEARNING
The Political Consequences of Scholarship in the Context of Judaism

Jacob Neusner

BM
75
$.N4835$
1985

Library of Congress Cataloging in Publication Data

Neusner, Jacob, 1932–
    The public side of learning.

    (AAR studies in religion ; 40)
    Includes index.
    1. Judaism—Study and teaching (Higher)—United
States—Addresses, essays, lectures. 2. Jews—History—
Study and teaching (Higher)—United States—
Addresses, essays, lectures. I. Title. II. Series: Studies in
religion (American Academy of Religion) ; no. 40.
BM75.N4835 1985 296'.07'11   85-8340
ISBN 0–87130–860–1 (alk. paper)
ISBN 0–87130–861–X (pbk. : alk paper)

Printed in the United States of America
on acid-free paper

For
Bernard Scharfstein

who, in a lifetime of scholarly publishing, has faithfully served every constituency of Judaic learning, with good will and commitment to the public interest. His record of public achievement proves the possibility of advancing the common cause of serious study, even among scholars who disagree on fundamental premises. He stands as an indictment of the empty hatreds and petty acts of contempt that characterize the contemporary scene of Judaic Studies. He proves that things do not have to be the way they are.

CONTENTS

PREFACE

In the past quarter-century the social foundations of Judaic studies changed radically. A new setting, the university, opened up for an old field of learning, the Jews, their religion, literature, history, society, culture, tradition. Pursued for many centuries under Jewish auspices and for Jewish purposes, Judaic studies confronted the challenges of the university. A vigorous debate on issues of social policy and the politics of culture now takes up the consequences of this striking shift in the institutional setting of a field of learning. In this book I wish to offer perspective on the public side of learning. Here I take up the political consequences of scholarship in the context of Judaism. In particular, Judaism as studied in a new setting, for new purposes, and by people who frame for themselves a new profession and a new definition has joined the community of academic learning. A new academic basis generates innovative paradigms of teaching and scholarship. In turn, established approaches come under unprecedented threat. Scholarly debates on fundamental issues get underway. So history replays old themes in new ways. The story of scholarship in every important field of humanistic and social scientific learning recounts the same tale of how an old paradigm reaches new expression. Now an old field in the brief span of a quarter-century has renewed itself. Why so? As the social foundations of learning shift, so we hear the echo in the noise of the earthquake. Seismologists of the intellect will want to measure that noise and tell us what it means. The foundations of a field of learning do not often shift beneath our feet.

My task in the book at hand is twofold. First, I wish to explain what I think has happened and why the changes matter. Second, I owe colleagues a decent explanation of the field as I wish to define it. I believe there are many such colleagues, not only in Judaic studies.

What I want to show, in particular, is how through reasoned debate we can transform "the enemy" into "the other," and "the other" into a lesson for the self. How so? In the academic study of religion we try to learn how to study as an object a topic that, for some of us, defines a subject, namely, what we are, a part of ourselves. We try, also, to find a way to study people different from ourselves, people who because we are what we are to us are others. I spell this out in Chapter 2. We want through the example of the study of religion to learn to describe, analyze, and interpret the other. When we do so, we may find out, further, how to make some sense of ourselves, as I try to do in Chapters 9 through 12. Now in insisting, in Chapter 2, that the study of religion constitutes a promising way of thinking about "the other," I have to demonstrate the power of conviction and intellect. That is to say, if I am right that the study of religion serves an important purpose of mind and intellect, then I have to show how what I learn leads me to make sense of what I find it difficult to understand.

Now if my conviction about how Judaic studies must take form is to prove sound, then I have to give evidence that the methods of the Enlightenment, with their stress on reason and civil discourse, skepticism, systematic doubt and rigorous argument, should apply here too. How so? This is the crux of the matter. It is my task to see "the enemy"—someone who differs or who is different—as merely an "other." I have to attempt to interpret the "enemy" as just another other, especially in Chapters 2, 6, and 7. So here I mean not to explain away, surely not to condemn, those who define the field in a different way. Saul Lieberman once said that while nonsense is nonsense, the history of nonsense is scholarship. So too, people who differ may see themselves as enemies, but the description, analysis, and interpretation of "enemies" for an intellectual and a scholar provide the mind's true therapy. That is so especially if the patient is legion, the stakes high, the issue the life of humanity in its several bonds and circles, the outcome the future of the social entity to which this scholar too adheres.

In the light of these remarks the papers that follow should make their own points and demand little reiteration.

In Part Two I place the study of Judaism into its larger framework of the study of religion. At the same time I go over the matters just now explained and spell out my interpretation of the remarkable reception accorded in some circles to my scholarly work. In Part Two I define what I conceive to be the character of the academic study of religion, then relate that field and its program to the university setting for Jewish learning, and, finally, spell out where I think Judaic studies in universities now stand after twenty-five years.

In Part Three I treat scholarly problems, rather than those of academic organization. I speak to two matters, first, the relationship between being Jewish and studying about Judaism, second, the scholarship that now emerges (and does not emerge) on account of the contemporary facts of the sociology of the field.

In Part Four I explain myself and my own work. My deepest faith lies in the power of reasonable people to make sense of what is going on, whether as scholars or as part of a broader public. In rational exchange of ideas, in civil discourse about matters of common concern, I do maintain there is a public interest to be served. I mean to serve that public interest. I know no better way to counter retrograde, parochial forces in Judaic studies than to force them too to state their case in the full light of day, by which I mean, in a fair and reasoned framework. Let one law, one reason, one mode of discourse apply to all. The enlightened forces of Enlightenment will sort things out. I have no doubt about the outcome.

Over the years I have tried through sequences of lectures to spin out a theory of the profession of the study of Judaism within the context of the academic study of religion. In working on these lectures my intent always is to say something both for and also beyond the occasion. Some sequences of lectures—those at Arizona State University, University of Rochester, and Emory University, for example—defined a single program of thought and in fact were meant to be continuous with one another. In other cases I prepared two or even three lectures for a single occasion, each written with the same detailed care as the others, then chose one of the three for delivery and set the rest aside for publication in an appropriate setting. That process is exemplified by the two Society for Biblical Literature plenary lectures for 1984 now printed in this book as Chapters 8 and 10. Another instance was provided by the invitation to deliver a plenary address for that same organization in 1979. This invitation precipitated "New Perspectives in the Study of Rabbinic Sources," which I never delivered but only printed, and "New Problems, New Solutions, Current Events in Rabbinic Studies," which I did give but later published. I therefore acknowledge the stimulus of many universities throughout the Western world that have accorded me the honor of a hearing over the past quarter-century. For someone so full of complaints as I am about the limitations of scholarly argument and discourse, I certainly cannot complain of not having received an ample hearing, except, of course, among the people to whom to begin with I mean to speak. But that is quite natural.

Four papers in this book come from already-published lectures or writings:

"Stranger at Home: The Task of Religious Studies": Beginning as the inaugural lecture of the Department of Religious Studies at Arizona State University on October 25, 1979, this lecture was printed in *The Academic Study of Judaism. Essays and Reflections. Third Series. Three Contexts of Jewish Learning* (New York: Ktav Publishing House, Inc., 1980).

"The New Setting for Jewish Learning and its Challenges": The keynote address at the Bernstein Conference on Jewish Studies, University of Rochester, February 22, 1976, this lecture was printed in *The Academic Study of Judaism. Essays and Reflections. Second Series* (New York: Ktav Publishing House, 1977), under its original title, "The New Setting for Jewish Learning: Towards a Theory of University Studies in Judaism."

"The Crisis of Jewish Learning in America": An address at the academic conference of the Hebrew College, Boston, Massachusetts, on

March 3, 1975, this paper was originally printed in *The Academic Study of Judaism. Essays and Reflections. Second Series* (New York: Ktav Publishing House, 1977), under the title, "Jewish Learning in America."

"Being Jewish and Studying about Judaism": Presented at the academic convocation in honor of the Cohen Professorship of Judaic Studies at Emory University on January 23, 1977, and marking the appointment of David R. Blumenthal as Cohen Professor; and given also at the Conference on Religious Studies and Cultural Pluralism at the University of Tennessee, Knoxville, on November 15–16, 1976, under the auspices of the Department of Religious Studies at the University of Tennessee, the Tennessee Committee for the Humanities, and the Society for Values in Higher Education, this lecture was printed in *The Academic Study of Judaism. Second Series.*

The other eight papers in this book as of this writing have not been published before. "An Interview" by William Novak will appear in the journal edited by him, *New Traditions*, No. 2, in 1985.

The remaining papers originated as follows:

"Judaic Studies in Universities. Toward the Second Quarter-Century": Lecture at Duke University on September 19, 1984, on the occasion of the announcement and celebration of the Smart Family/Terry Sanford Endowment Fund for a Smart Family Professorship in Judaic Studies in the College of Arts and Sciences at Duke University.

"Toward the Disciplinary Expansion of Judaic Studies": A lecture at Northwestern University on December 9, 1984.

"Taking Things Apart to See How They Work" was prepared for use as the third annual plenary address, "How My Mind Has Changed," for the Society of Biblical Literature meeting in Chicago, Illinois, in 1984. It was printed in the seminar papers for that meeting but not presented orally.

"Methods for the Study of Religion": A panel-paper at the American Academy of Religion meeting, presented on December 9, 1984.

J. N.

25 Kislev 5745
The first day of Hanukkah.
December 19, 1984.
The light shines ever brighter.

Part One

THE PUBLIC SIDE OF LEARNING

1. SCHOLARSHIP, CULTURE, AND POLITICS

Scholars maintain the pretense that they deal in mere facts, certainties remote from the upheavals of the common culture. Scholarship takes place in a utopian realm of reason, where people make up their minds on scholarly issues only after dispassionately sorting out reasonable alternatives. What scholars say, therefore, makes a journey from mind to disembodied mind, unimpeded by the petty obstacles of emotion or interest, the stuff of the sordid life of ordinary folk. In their sealed pockets of paradise, scholars imagine, they live out in intellect charmed and providential lives.

That fantasy survives even the locative realities of scholars' everyday lives among themselves, in their departments and universities, in their professional associations and in their journals. If, as Aristotle says, man is a political animal, then so far as scholars work with one another in departments, speak to one another in books and articles, and propose to debate with one another and change minds—so far as scholars do the work of scholarship—they undertake a wholly political task. They carry out that task under conditions entirely familiar to political scientists. They therefore make up their minds and change them not solely or even primarily in response to reasoned argument unimpeded by social and political considerations. In all, they sort out facts in a framework of many dimensions, not all of them defined by reason, and not a few of them framed by emotion, self-interest, cherished prejudices, family relationships, and long-nurtured grudges and hostilities of both a personal and a theological character. So far as scholars flourish in this world and do its work, they are political animals. And why not, since, so far as scholarship differs from gibberish, at stake in scholarly inquiry always and invariably are important issues, things that matter to people.

The public side of learning (a phrase I owe to my co-worker, William Scott Green) makes of important scholars public figures, people whom others discuss. Under enlightened circumstances, a name will stand for a position. A person will embody a viewpoint or a method. Under ordinary conditions, however, names refer to saints or demons. Scholarly issues commonly serve as a mask for personal animosities. The quest for truth and in sight thus turns up something rather more human. That is hardly to be regretted. Why not? Because scholarship matters. At stake are important issues of contemporary life. The alternative premise is that scholarship does not tell us anything we want to know or need to take to heart. The vivid and even emotional character of scholarly debate, now as in the past, validates the former of the two premises. The demise of entire scholarly fields shows us what happens when the latter premise proves valid, when people stop caring.

Now when we consider the public side of learning and wish to know and understand in some detail how scholarship responds to contemporary concerns, we best turn to specific fields of learning. In the sociology and politics of a field of study we discern what is happening in our own day, even when women and men speak of ancient times and dead issues. So far as we take to heart the character of public debate about erudite matters, we grasp the truth that scholarship defines a life of creativity. Human knowledge makes its way not around but through the human heart. So public discourse may bring to our ears only gossip, trivialization of great issues of culture through their reduction to the clash of personalities, evidences of the degradation of the public interest in the issues of learning through the assassination of the character of the public figures of learning. Yet while public discourse produces evidence not of reasoned exchange of ideas but of politics and the clash of personalities, public discourse is the lifeblood, the fresh air of learning.

So we might as well speak boldly and plainly about how matters really are. In that way we gain access to the issues not only of politics and personalities, but also of society and culture. How so? If we recognize what happens in the public side of learning and take to heart the political consequences of scholarship, we gain access to that other aspect of matters, the one that counts. I mean that by seeing what is political, we can grasp what of the intellect endures in the social imagination of groups, so too in their politics. When we know that the forms of scholarly debate conceal personal envy and disappointment, long-nurtured grievance, theological and scholastic hatreds, we may learn to recognize the authentic from the spurious in scholarly debate. We may, in other words, discern the real, the intellectual issues only when we know that, to begin with, scholarship expresses more aspects of the scholar's heart and mind, soul and intellect, than scholars in general are prepared to confess.

One powerful motive for the politicization of scholarly discourse derives from deeply held and fiercely defended public convictions. Discoveries that disorient a field may disturb an individual. But approaches and viewpoints that call into question the political or social or religious foundations of a social entity—a nation, a religious group—will produce response far more consequential than private hatreds and personal vilification. After all, the one who hates at worst will write a mean review. But sooner or later, he goes the way of all flesh. Such a one just takes the low road out of life, leaving behind the ruins of whatever good name that person in public attempted to construct. But when the inner life of a whole group comes under perceived (whether or not real) attack, and when the attack takes intellectual and scholarly form, then one or two timely deaths will make no difference. The war will go on and on.

Institutions of learning then will find themselves drawn into the battle. Libraries will lock away proscribed books. Journals will not review forbidden publications or even print articles submitted by authors on the index. Learned articles will cite only approved publications and omit all reference to disapproved ones, so that bibliographies frame the battleground. Scholarly organizations will form around one party's viewpoint and keep out the other's. Boycotts conducted not by individual writers or bibliographers or librarians but by entire universities, even by whole countries, will bring to full expression the intense hatred at hand. Obviously, when these things take place, we confront the less benign face of the public side of learning. But it is one that enlightens in its way. Even in boycott, institutionalized hatred, collective irrationality, even in the demonization of the one that holds the wrong views and in the humiliation of the party that raises the tough questions, we see an important truth of scholarship.

If we do not perceive that truth, moreover, we shall gain little from the scholarship of the age. For, as is clear, we shall be unable to sort things out and to recognize legitimate and reasoned debate about issues when and where such debate does take place. And it does take place. Scholarship does flourish. Books worth reading do get written. New generations do come forward to carry on the long line of learning upon which civilization draws sustenance and strength. So the political consequences of scholarship do not dictate the future. Nor do they even impede present work. They define merely part of the setting in which scholars do their work and deserve a measure of attention on that account. But attention differs from obsession. In this book I do not propose to settle scores or mainly make points. I wish, rather, to do my best as a scholar to explain the circumstance of a field today ripped apart by politics of a theological and cultural character and to explain, as best I can, how I understand my own place in the formation of a fresh consensus within that field.

Clearly, the field of the study of Judaism provides a useful example of the dimensions of the public life of learning. Why so?

First, the study of Judaism carries scholars to fiercely debated issues and cherished convictions. So we may expect to find interesting cases for the study of the political consequences of scholarship.

Second, the field as a whole is small, with only a few important centers. So if we see evidence of a holy war in progress, we need not waste much time counting the troops on either side. They are few and easy to recognize.

At issue, third, we find questions familiar to a broad range of humanistic fields, questions fought out and long ago settled in most other fields. So the issues, acutely divisive rather than chronically troubling, do not emerge from an alien world, which we can never hope to understand. On the contrary, in an area of learning conducted under both parochial and public auspices, under the control in some areas of a state-church, in other areas of theological bodies, and in still other areas of academic professors, we may find a latter-day case of a quite familiar paradigm.

We can easily explain what has happened to precipitate the battles of the hour. Specifically, the institutional setting for the study of Judaism and the Jews used to find a capacious place entirely within the frame of Jewish sponsorship and participation. Jews studied Judaism with Jews. Jews taught Judaism to Jews. Jewish institutions of Jewish learning, both in the State of Israel, and in Western Europe, as well as in America and Canada, defined nearly the entire setting for Jewish studies. About a quarter-century ago, however, an unprecedented and essentially unexpected setting for academic learning opened its doors to Judaic studies. The universities of the USA and Canada, as well as Western Europe, South Africa, South America, and Australia, for diverse reasons and in various ways made a place for aspects of Judaic studies. The new institutional setting by its very character imposed a different set of intellectual, social, and political conditions on the age-old field of learning at hand. These I spell out in Chapters 2 and 6. Some who entered that new world tried to learn about those conditions and respond to them. I explain how I did so in my career, as Chapters 9 through 12 indicate. Many did not. One battle got under way. Many in the familiar world of Jewish institutions of Judaic studies chose to reject out of hand the new setting and treat as alien all who entered it; a handful did not. So yet a second battle, on a different field, began. But the real war would be fought not on narrowly institutional grounds but in a far broader field altogether. This third battle—a war about ideas—is explained in Chapters 4, 7, and 8.

At issue in this war was and is what is at issue in every war: cherished beliefs, long-held convictions, the ideas around which entire societies build their worlds, the ideals for which people live and are prepared to die. So here too, at issue in the end (at least as I see it) were ideas and ideals. And by definition these are intellectual. Whether we now frame matters in theological terms or in historical ones, the issue will remain the same. It concerns ideas. Specifically, Jewish learning now confronts the issues of the Enlightenment. What the Enlightenment stands for is skepticism, clear and acerbic thought. That mode of thought and learning insists upon self-consciousness, rejects cant and excessive belief, destroys through ridicule the bastions of credulity and gullibility that have long endured. The Enlightenment in its totally secular form in fact had never reached the realm of Judaic studies. No door had ever opened to it.

For as a secular movement of mind, the Enlightenment, in particular as it reached full expression in the formation of social sciences, never made room for the special pleading of this political entity or that religion. All worthwhile learning aimed, as now it aims, at discovering the rules by which all groups equally conduct their lives. Diverse religions, at home with ethnographers, theologians, and historians of this and that, therefore viewed with alarm those who asked how religions in fact comprise religion.

Long-standing arguments could readily dispose of doubt within and hostile challenge without. But what is a religious group to say to someone who wishes to understand that group not alone in its own terms but in categories alien to itself? Religious groups invariably posit a special relationship to God or claim to be unique. That is what makes religions religion. Then how is a religious community to confront scholarship that asks questions of generalization addressed to people who claim to be different, therefore destined by God for difference? These givens of social science and of humanistic learning as generally carried on in universities came into conflict with a different set of givens.

The other set of intensely divisive issues, in the case of Jewish learning, derived from Judaism. In the religious version Judaism represents God's will; the Jews constitute God's chosen people or (in a more enlightened form) God's first love. In the secular version the Jews' diverse histories, here and there, constitute a single and unitary history, a continuous and linear nation or people. So (1) the Jews form a continuity. They (2) have survived (as they now must continue to survive). They survive while others have not survived. So (3) their survival marks them as unique, and (4) the continuous history they have written for themselves demonstrates for all to see that (5) they uniquely survive. So while—in this secularized version of religious belief—the Jews are not the chosen people, they still are unique. Or, to put matters as a witty rabbi has stated them, "The secular Jews know there is no God, but they are sure the Jews are His chosen people." It comes down to the same thing. Whether the study of Judaism and of the Jews served theological purposes, as in rabbinical seminaries in the USA and Western Europe, or in national ones as in the State of Israel, the purpose and premise remained one and the same.

But in universities scholars take as data, demanding dispassionate investigation, those cherished convictions of chosenness, continuity, survival, linear and continuous history, and uniqueness, that in the Jewish institutions of Judaic studies defined the very ground of being, the ultimate commitment of learning, as of the Jews' life beyond the school. So at the foundations of the war lie not mere institutional rivalries and petty patriotism of a transient sort. At issue is something important, public, and political. That is why I claim that if people wish to gain perspective on the public side of learning and examine the impact upon scholarship of the aspect of humanity as a political animal, what has happened in Judaic studies matters.

Part Two

JUDAISM IN THE CONTEXT
OF THE STUDY OF RELIGION

2. STRANGER AT HOME
The Task of Religious Studies

I

We inaugurate a new Department of Religious Studies because many people share the conviction that such a department, working on such a subject, not only belongs in the university curriculum. They hold that the curriculum is impoverished without the academic study of religions—so poor, indeed, that even in these days of poverty for higher education, the administration and faculty of this University have agreed to do what they have done. Since for twenty years I have made my life and my living in the field of Religious Studies and have known no other life or living, I take this event as a statement of confidence in what my generation of scholars set out to do. But inaugurating a new Department also presents us with an important challenge. We must use this occasion to ask ourselves, once more, what we think we are doing in the study of religions and why we claim it to be so important.

Let me start with the end, the picture of the last graduation day at Brown University. Then our students passed before us, and we before them, in a curious pattern of march and counter-march by which we fill an otherwise empty graduation rite. As the students walked past the faculty, I reflected on how in some past years my colleagues and I had taught so few, but this year so many, of these students. I asked myself whether we had made a significant contribution to their education and growth into adulthood, for that is the social task which, quite rightly I think, society assigns to the liberal arts colleges and universities of this country. And as we of the faculty walked past the students, I felt I could look into their eyes with a measure of pride in what my colleagues and I had given them these past four years.

This inauguration lecture, like that graduation ceremony, is a time to reflect on our tasks and the worth of our work to our students and to society. It is a time to think about our responsibility. For we bear a three-part responsibility. We (1) teach (2) a particular subject to (3) students. Here are three elements: that we *teach*, that we teach *students*, that we teach students *some particular thing* in such a way that they learn an accurate and responsible account of a subject worth knowing. If we pay no attention to who sits before us, we do not teach. If we do not tell them anything important, we waste their time. We are educators, scholars. But we also are models of a particular sort of mind, a distinctive kind of response to the world of learning.

If we do not ask ourselves tough questions about the intellectual and social worth of what we teach, we declare ourselves both intellectually bankrupt and socially irresponsible. This we cannot do while asking society for its children to teach and for its resources to support our teaching. I find myself impatient, therefore, when told that any subject, whether religion or biology, is "intrinsically" interesting. I am prepared to concede that all subjects are intrinsically interesting. But I do not know what value there is in such a concession. For we have to make choices, and so does society. It will not do to commend everything and decline nothing. We must exercise taste and judgment. We must also explain the result. That is self-evidently not an argument in favor of a pragmatic or narrowly utilitarian approach to learning. But neither is it going to give comfort to scholars who disdain to teach, teachers who prefer to preach, or faculties which become lazy, unresponsive, and indifferent to their tasks both in education and in scholarship.

No one can hope that there are lasting answers to the question, Why should I know the things which you are telling me? But the generation of teachers and scholars which does not try to answer fails both those who came before and those who are to come.

II

The starting point of any answer should be the educational result we hope to achieve. That result will be in two parts, first, with reference to students in general, whatever their majors, and second, with reference to majors in our field.

The former group is far more important than the latter, for the reason I implied at the outset. Our interest is to provide something of cultural and intellectual value to a wide variety of students, to serve the entire community of our university. Given the vocational choices which govern curricular decisions made by the generality of students everywhere, we are not going to see massive numbers of students in our more specialized courses. They will study other things. Most of them will not earn a living from what they learn from us, nor will what we have to teach in concrete ways make them more useful in their chosen business, profession, or calling. My own impression, moreover, is that students who come to us from mathematics and the natural sciences tend to be more engaging, because, by the nature of things, in the world about which we speak, they also are both uninformed and rather unformed. Since my own university has impressive numbers of students in pre-medical studies as well as in engineering, mathematics, and the natural sciences, and very large numbers of other students who plan to become lawyers or to go to business school, I must ask myself questions of purpose in a context quite different from that in which colleagues in biology or applied mathematics explain why someone should want to know what they teach.

Our situation in the study of religions is characteristic of the humanities in general. It is our task to shape Religious Studies within the humanities in such a way that they win the attention of students engaged by other things, and cause them to be willing to learn what we have to teach. It is another to teach something worthy of attention. Ours is the work of doing both. Yet it remains to observe that the generality of our students see us for one or two or three courses, while they pursue their major field for eight or ten or twelve courses. The result is that Religious Studies, for the main part of their student constituency, take the form of courses which survey a fair amount of material for a sizable number of students, courses which meet a requirement, and from which students themselves demand somewhat more than they do of their majors: to tell them whatever they should know, while, so to speak, we stand on one foot (if not on our heads).

But this demand is an opportunity and a challenge. It requires us to ask, Among the many important and pressing things I wish to share out of what I know, what are the most urgent? Every time we plan a course, we select the few things we can manage in the twelve or fourteen weeks we have. This act of selection, which begins when we claim to do our subject for more than its "intrinsic" interest, continues in the many acts of selection by which we frame our courses, the topics of our lectures, the readings we put into students' hands.

Before proceeding to outline these urgent matters, I call to mind that other, rather select group of students, our majors in Religious Studies. Since these students only occasionally plan to enter the priesthood, ministry, rabbinate, or other religious vocations and careers, in their vocational character they are not so different from the students whom we serve in a few survey or general courses. Moreover, most of them take so wide a variety of courses within Religious Studies that nearly every course they elect also turns out to be elementary. If an advanced course is one which demands a prerequisite of some other, prior course, we almost always teach beginners. For an examination of catalogues yields very few second or third courses in our field. Many of these allegedly advanced courses turn out to be just as elementary as the others. There may be an "introductory" course, required of all students. But, commonly, in no way does such a course pretend to introduce all the other courses students may take. It hardly lays down foundations on which the other courses within the departmental curriculum are going to build. Proof? There rarely are prerequisites. Our field is too specialized, too diverse in its methods. It follows that the bulk of our teaching serves students who ask absolutely fundamental questions, one of which must always be, Why are you telling me these things? Why should I know them? How shall I be changed because I know them?

III

We live in an age of intense faith and of utter indifference about religions. Our work is important both to the faithful and to those for whom religious belief and behavior bear no this-worldly interest whatsoever. Our work is not to reshape the faith of the faithful, nor to kindle interest in the uninterested. It is different. When we say we stand at a distance from the subject, claim to be objective about the "truth-claims" of the religions we study, or solemnly affirm that we do not serve, or violate, the interests of organized religion or of atheism, our protestations are true but miss the point. What we do in general is simply not suitably described or explained within the frame of reference expressed in terms of faith or unfaith, commitment or doubt, even concern or unconcern about the subject. What we do is to try to interpret the phenomenon of religions as a force in human life.

To answer the question, Why Religious Studies? we have to ask another: What do people *not* know, if they do not know about and understand religions? What can they *not* explain and of what can they not make sense? Phrased in this way, the question answers itself. For religion is so powerful a force in the contemporary world that without knowledge of religion we scarcely can understand the daily newspapers. A fair example of what happens when people do not know how to make sense of the power of religions in contemporary life is our country's difficulty in understanding the Islamic revolution in Iran, not to mention the Judaic revolution in the State of Israel, the Protestant army of Northern Ireland, the Roman Catholic revolution in Poland and in Latin America, the Christian army of Lebanon, the tragedy at Jonestown, and many continuing evidences of the vitality of religious belief—sometimes healthy, sometimes perverse.

There is of course a bias against religion as a force in culture and psychology. This is surely one possible way of thinking about the character and meaning of society and of life. It holds religion to be dying, a holdover from another age. It therefore claims that religion does not require study. Those of us who find religion an exceptionally interesting phenomenon of society and culture, imagination and the heart, can do little to overcome this bias. But it *is* a bias, for it rests upon the will to wish religion away, not upon the perception that religion has gone away. In fact, much of the world as we know it is shaped by the formation of society and culture around religious beliefs, by the way in which people refer to religions to make their choices about how they will live. These beliefs and choices invoke particular modes of supernaturalism, distinctive expressions of revelation. A country governed by a president who speaks of a personal experience of conversion had better understand the meaning of religious conversion. A nation in which institutions of religion exercise vast influence over citizens' political and cultural decisions is not wise to deny that religion is a formative force in contemporary life. Whether or not people want religions to exercise that power, they do. In fact, religions not only speak about supernatural powers, they, too, constitute powerful forces in this world.

So it is a matter of fact that if people do not understand the character of religions, they cannot make sense of much that happens in the world today. Nor need we dwell upon a still more obvious fact. To understand where humankind has been, to make sense of the heritage of world civilization, the transcendant side of the human imagination and of society and culture constitutes a definitive dimension. There is no understanding of humanity without the confrontation with the religious heritage and hope, whatever may be our judgment of the value of the heritage and the hope. So far as universities propose to teach how to interpret the world in which we live, organizing courses and departments of Religious Studies is a perfectly natural way of teaching what must be taught.

IV

To this point in the argument I have tried to explain two of the three elements mentioned earlier, spelling out whom we teach and explaining that we teach, that is, transmit facts, ideas, and insight about important things. We have now to try to speak of the particular things we do in Departments of Religious Studies. It is axiomatic that we do not produce more faithful, or less faithful, Christians, Jews, Moslems, Buddhists, and the like. But it is equally clear that we do claim to attempt to explain these powerful forces in human culture which we call religions.

The task of explanation is accomplished through three distinct approaches to learning—history, philosophy, and social science. Each approach to the study of religions is indispensible. None exhausts the possible approaches to the work. In the area of history, we ask about the role and development of diverse religions within diverse cultures, within the life of various peoples, regions, and territories. Work in this area tends to rely upon literary evidence, for example, holy books, although archaeologists have begun to teach us to take seriously non-literary evidence. In the area of philosophy we analyze the language and claims about truth put forward in various religions; we ask about the ethics laid forth, and speak of the perennial issues of religious truth phrased in terms applicable to any culture. In social scientific approaches we inquire into the social setting and impact of a religion, on the one side, and into religions' psychological meaning, the place of religion in the life of the imagination and emotion, on the other. The enduring classics of theory of religions, for instance, the works of Freud, Weber, and Durkheim, have come from the fields of psychology and sociology of religions. Nor is the study of religions complete without the learning of anthropologists, who, like historians of religion, reach out to alien people, to people who, though living in the present, are foreign to our age, speaking in a strange language, about things we know not what. Anthropologists teach us to understand in common human terms the system, structure, and order of this alien world in our midst.

In this rapid account of the main disciplines of Religious Studies, we have also to catalogue the sorts of data to be analyzed by scholars of the field. Since human beings express transcendent impulses in every medium of access, scholars of religion have to teach themselves to recognize and hear these expressions wherever they occur. That is why the study of literature of the present and past, of art of today and yesterday, of music, drama, dance, poetry, cinema, as much as of sociology and anthropology, makes formidable contributions to the description and interpretation of religions. Nor may we omit notice of the important lessons to be learned from specialists in fields in which data of religions play only a peripheral part. It is not possible to understand the religions of the West without studying Western civilization, just as one cannot understand the civilizations of the West without intimate knowledge of religious institutions and expectations. So we come to our colleagues in history for assistance in our work. Political science, with its insight into how religious convictions and origins play a role in social and political behavior, provides ample data for the examination of religion as a vital and powerful force in contemporary life. Since art, music, and literature give access to what is happening in the soul of a society, there is no way to ignore the sizable work to be done in these departments of learning.

By now the picture is obvious. When we ask what we do in the study of religions, we discover ourselves in the very center of a field of learning which, at its foundations, is interdisciplinary and cross-cultural. It relies so heavily upon so wide a range of disciplines as to be declared the quintessential form of humanistic learning. Religious Studies cast a net over land and sea and everywhere find treasure. Whether or not there is a discipline distinctive to the study of religion I do not know. I am certain that there is no discipline of the academic curriculum in humanistic and social studies which Religious Studies can afford to neglect. This is surely so if we wish to understand this protean force, this ubiquitous thing, religion. For to study religion is to study humanity in its full humanness: integrated and whole, but frail, vulnerable, full of fantasies and fears, and in perpetual quest. It is no wonder that one religion finds its evocative symbol in a criminal in his death throes, and another finds its vindication in the very suffering of its communicants. In these ways and in others Christianity and Judaism, among the religions of humanity, express that vulnerability and frailty which, through religions, humankind has sought to express and to overcome.

V

Thus far I have explained what I believe to be the remarkable power of Religious Studies: first, their capacity to make their own nearly the entire spectrum of humanistic, and most of the social scientific, disciplines of learning, and, second, their reason for studying virtually every kind of expression of our humanness. But the power of the field is also its problem and its pathos. If we attempt to do so much, shall we not do most of it superficially, and the rest incompetently? That question by no means is to be dismissed. When, years ago, our department searched for a scholar in the social scientific approach to the study of religions, we found it difficult to locate an appropriate social scientist willing to join us. The more intelligent ones preferred to be sociologists of religion in departments of sociology. The sociologists who wanted to join us did not find academic sociology engaging. And the work of both sorts—with its stress on counting and measuring things—seemed to us not very interesting anyhow. But whatever the difficulties, religious studies depend, perhaps more than the study of most other humanistic subjects, upon help from colleagues. Indeed, we constantly refer to colleagues in other disciplines, both to teach us how they do their work, and to guide us in doing our own. The interdependence of religious studies with other disciplines of the humanities and social sciences is a powerful argument for the formation of a distinct department, such as this one. But it is a still stronger argument that, once the department has discovered its identity and purpose, its task is to reach out to colleagues with an interest in the thing we study and with much to teach us about it and about how to study it.

It is one thing to say that we are interested in everything. But it is quite another to specify the things that, in general, scholars in Religious Studies do well, and to confess the things that, in general, they tend to do poorly. So any account of the field as it takes up its duties in a new department of Religious Studies must address this very question. I see four principal sins of Religious Studies in the past twenty years.

The problems we tend to treat expertly are familiar ones. They derive from Western civilization. The kinds of sources we handle with skill normally are literary. The issues in the study of religions we confront with confidence arise from the Christian and Western philosophical perspectives upon religious experience and thought. In other words we do well what we know, less well what we do not. So while we may rightly claim to be interested in everything, we are disingenuous if we offer that claim at face value. This is the first of four sins of Religious Studies. The field's diffuse character conceals its cultural sameness, its origins in Protestant divinity schools. To observe that the curriculum of a fair number of departments, particularly in smaller, church-related colleges, replicates too accurately the principal interests of divinity faculties, is to bring no news. To point out that an alternative in both scholarship and teaching has yet to be worked out and made to stick is another matter.

Our vision of the subject remains pretty much what it was. We have the breadth of concern which is the virtue of the Protestant conscience. But we also exhibit the incapacity to attain critical self-consciousness, the conviction of majorities that how we see things is pretty much how they are, which is the vice. The caring for all things is formed into a utensil of one shape only, by limited sympathy. No one has to choose a position of entire relativity of values to notice that, in the study of religions, we tend to bring a rather limited program of interests and concerns. That is why some, who work on religions essentially unlike Protestant Christianity, turn to anthropology for categories of inquiry. We find the narrowly theological, intellectual definition of issues of Religious Studies to be of limited utility. That is why others turn to approaches borrowed from other data, for instance, structuralism as a mode of interpreting ritual. The inherited, philosophical categories of the field do not present a viable hermeneutic for religions as they are practiced outside of this country's Protestant Churches and culture.

A further trait of the field derives, if by somewhat remote connection, from yet another strength of Protestant culture: the power to respond to the events of the moment. It is its capacity to remain relevant to a changing world, to address each hour afresh, which has made Protestant culture so functional to the industrial West. A natural attitude of mind in our field is to respond quickly and relevantly to what happens in ways which some of us, out of more "traditional" cultures, find admirable. At the same time Religious Studies as a field tend to go from hula-hoop to frisbee, taking as evanescent slogans ideas which the framer means to be handled very seriously indeed. After twenty years in the field of Religious Studies I have learned to approach with measured enthusiasm the intellectually-salvific theories of the moment. When I find at the American Academy of Religion pretty much a single slogan sweeping from one section to the next—whether it is "the social construction of reality," or "phenomenology," or "structuralism," or even something so specific as black, women's, or Jewish perspectives on Religious Studies—I go back to my room and watch television. For there at least the fads are an honest way to make a living.

What is wrong with the perpetual faddism and sloganeering of the field is not that slogans contain no truth or convey no insight. It is that in our faddism we forget the roots of the academic study of religions. What is new in the marketplace of ideas turns out to be a repackaging of what is old. The second sin of the field thus is academic consumerism. How many steps do we take, after all, from Durkheim to Douglas? And how far a journey do we travel from Weber to Bellah and Geertz? The classicism of the Judaic tradition and of the Roman Catholic form of Christianity—to name accessible modes of belief—has yet to make its contribution to the shaping of attitudes of mind in our nascent discipline. Only in preserving the tension between the claims of the exciting new and the doubts of the experienced old shall we succeed in retaining some sort of balance and prudence in our intellectual venture.

The methodological diffuseness of the field, which is its strength, exacts a price in an absence of critical self-consciousness, on the one side, and an excess of contemporaneity, on the other. It tends to yield yet another good thing which also is bad: a general education. In those universities which lack programs in Western civilization, the study of two subjects tends to take their place: history, in the form of the general survey course, and religious studies, in the form of the introductory course, e.g., to Catholicism, Protestantism, and Judaism, or to the religions of the West, or, still grander, to the religions of the whole world. Surely it is an act of responsibility and of courage for our faculties to undertake these kinds of courses. Student response as well as collegial approval (for others do not wish to tread where we happily proceed) gratifies and rewards us. If, because of its integrated and wide-ranging topicality, the study of religions serves as a kind of general education, it also replicates the dubious intellectual traits of general education. Our general, introductory courses—often the only ones our students elect—leave the impression of breadth, when they make a superficial mark; appear to speak of important things, when they raise issues which are merely relevant; and evoke the language of eternity, but speak, in the end, of how we feel today. These are bitter judgments. They judge as much what I do as anyone else.

The third sin is that in our teaching we are mere generalists, when we should be specialists speaking in accessible, general terms—a very different thing. We talk about too many things. This is bad not merely because about most we come armed only with our impressions. It also is bad because we lose the power to criticize ourselves, even to distinguish bad from good in our own thought and understanding. I am unhappy, for example, at how little effort goes into the careful and sympathetic reading of the texts of alien religions. It is as if we wish to get the gist of an ancient tablet without making sense of the glyphs of the alien alphabet. It cannot be done. Meaning must be expressed in words. Words come in one language or another, governed by a specific syntax and intimate grammar of thought and idiomatic expression. Those of us who teach what is not commonly familiar, because we tend to be embarrassed at the alienness of our texts, leap over the specificities into a common language of thought. We chatter in a kind of intellectual Esperanto which no one really uses at all.

We have not figured out how to teach some one or two texts, in a given course, which will say things beyond themselves, yet distinctive and particular to themselves. It is exceedingly difficult to find the modalities between technical gibberish (which would then place us in graduate seminars of philology) and insufferable banality (which leaves us right where we are). To put matters more simply: I do not yet know the way which leads from telling my students about King Upupalupu to informing them that "Deep down, people really are good, anyhow." In the interstices between knowing how to read and interpret a text or some other datum of religion (a play, a dance, a rite, a prayer), and knowing how to talk to the concerns of the hour and of the particular age through which the students now pass, lies that kind of teaching which, right now, is difficult to define: teaching students something worth knowing.

The fourth and last sin is most serious. No indictment of Religious Studies as an academic field can fail to charge that we have played our full part in the destruction of the study of foreign languages in America. If I have to point to the single indefensible achievement of our field (it is no defense that we did not do it all by ourselves), it is the propagation of the notion that we can understand what is alien without learning the language of the alien. Our sin is not merely the absence of requirements that our majors learn some language relevant to their studies of religions. It is a failure at the very center of our mission which allows our students to assume that they understand things to which, in fact, they do not even gain access.

Our work is to make what is strange into something human, to teach how to make sense, in *its* alien terms, of what some among us too soon make their own. The study of religions, when not wholly subjective, and therefore not academic to begin with, is the study of the religious life of others. It is not the religious life of the teacher of a given classroom or of every student in that classroom. The other, to be understood, cannot be reduced to ourselves. *We have to allow the other to be different—and then to confront and attempt to overcome the difference without dissolving it.* It is no news to declare that the work of the humanities is to examine the diversity of human experience and to ask what is human about humankind. But how are we to confront diversity and take difference seriously, when we do not even know that other people talk of things we know not what, in languages which to us are gibberish? The first step in any humanistic venture of learning must be to allow the other to be alien, yet to seek for what is like ourselves in the alien. The final step is to understand more than that the stranger is in ourselves. It is to realize, also, that we are in the stranger.

Now it is one thing to tell people things. It is another for people to experience them. I can think of no more direct, experiential encounter with the specific issues of the humanities than in learning a foreign language. For the beginning of that process of learning is to seek in the language we want to learn analogies and metaphors for the language we already know. But the end of that learning is when the language we want to learn takes on its own reality in our ears, eyes, and mouths, so that we make the alien tongue into our own. When we deprive our students of the opportunity to enter into an alien language, we deprive ourselves of the occasion to teach what we really know, which is more than what our students already know.

In reading finals in my courses I am struck by how many could have been written without taking my courses at all. Students do not hear, because they do not understand that we are not telling them things they already know, even when we may say words they already have heard. I am astonished at how much which to me seems fresh and new enters the students' ears in accord with patterns of thought and definitions of issues established far away and long before they come to me. Many times I try to say, "If you think you already know this, you are not understanding what I am saying." But where can I evoke that consciousness of *not* understanding which must precede the process of seeking understanding among people who have never heard in their lives a foreign word or an alien thought? For students must first learn to be strangers to themselves, before they can see the given as chosen and new, and themselves as free to make choices.

To be sure, this country is not a monolingual society. Each region is rich in its own culture and speech. All parts of the country benefit from the presence of communities which speak some language other than American English. But we tend to ignore what we do not understand and to suppose that we all say pretty much the same thing in the same way. In fact we talk past one another, each about something the other could not make sense of, even if it were explained.

We in the humanities vindicate our work because it teaches people how to think. The very absence of a vocational tie between our subject and the students' future justifies what we do. Yet if we are training minds, then alongside those skills in clear thinking and accurate expression which we seek to cultivate belongs the direct experience of the alien which comes only in learning a text in its own language. It is not merely because when students never encounter the language other people use they do not do the hard work of cultural interpretation. It is more especially because of something more particular to our own field. When students do not realize, in their own direct experience of the alien, that nearly everything we have reaches us in a labor of translation and mediation, they do not grasp what is at the core of the study of religions. At the center of our intellectual enterprise is this same work—the translation and mediation of alien experience. This is what the study of a foreign language, properly carried out, makes available: the struggle to understand, to make sense in our language, of what is not our own.

VI

What makes the study of religions difficult is also what makes the work important. The principal difficulty is that the students all take for granted they know that about which we are talking. Nearly all of them come from one or another of the religious traditions of the West. Many of them have strong opinions on religions and on questions of theology. So they think they know already what we have to tell them. That is the challenge. But it also is what makes our work important. For, as I shall now argue, the crucial thing we can give, which our students badly need, is the encounter with the unfamiliar in what they take for granted. We can show them that what they think they know contains much yet to be learned. We can demonstrate that the absolute, wholly familiar given of life—that matter of religion—contains within itself a great many choices. Once we persuade them that, within religious expressions, people make important choices about the sort of society and culture they will sustain and the kind of people they will build, we provide them with an insight into their own most urgent task, namely, to learn how to make choices about things which seem settled and decided, to see as strange and new, requiring reflection and thought, what has all the time appeared familiar, routine, and closed. In the experience of discovering the familiar to be strange and to require analysis, our students undergo the experience of intellectual maturing which prepares them for a deeper, inner movement toward adulthood. My claim therefore is not a small one. I argue that the academic study of religions, because of its particular character, presents a splendid opportunity for our students to experience in intellectual terms what in fact is their most profound and pressing personal responsibility: the discovery of self, the engagement with their own individuality. What we do is relevant, in the deepest sense, to the students' task of attaining adulthood.

Let me explain. It is this matter of the encounter with what is not our own which, when our work succeeds, we may declare to be educational success and, when our work does not succeed, we recognize as failure. At the outset I argued that the reason the study of religions belongs in the center of the curriculum is that religions are a powerful and ubiquitous force in humankind. But what it is about religions which we need to master for the sake of useful knowledge remains to be stated. This is to be explained in two aspects. I have, first, to say why we think our students in particular ought to know about the things we teach. I must explain, second, why the society and community we serve ought to know them.

Since our students in the main are late adolescents, our work is defined by the psychological and emotional context of that age-group, as much as by its vocational or even cultural aspirations. Indeed, in any group of university students, however carefully selected. I am inclined to wonder whether many even *have* vocational and cultural goals. But all of them are engaged by how they feel, what they think about themselves, and what their peer group thinks about them.

Now the power of the study of religions is that, in our society, we speak of kinds of familiar experiences. It is difficult to grow up in America without knowing that there are churches and synagogues, religious myths and symbols of various kinds, to which various folk respond in diverse ways. There are experiences of religious conversion and rebirth, rites of birth and puberty, teachings about what one may do and must not do, and institutions for the expression and embodiment of all of these things. It follows that our students know that about which we are talking when we speak about religions. That is our richest asset. But it also is the most formidable obstacle to teaching our students something worth their knowing.

To explain, I must emphasize that what young people approaching maturity require is the capacity finally to surpass themselves, leaving childish things, while retaining the heritage of family, home, and love. They have to learn how to make their own what others have made for them, so to enter, finally, into the life of maturity and responsibility. They come to us as dependents upon their parents. They leave to take up their own careers. In the four years they spend with us, we have to guide them from dependence to independence. It is this supererogatory work of helping in the process of maturing which, in many instances, is our richest gift to our students.

Now if in intellect we can confront them with an authentic experience of attaining self-consciousness and of critically, thoughtfully evaluating what they think they already know in the encounter with what they do not know—the "alien experience" to which I referred earlier— then we allow for a controlled experiment of maturing. That is to say, through their intellectual labor we guide them in paths which, by analogy and metaphor, lead where life demands they go.

To state the matter simply: they already know about religions, more commonly, "their" religion. But they do not know what they know, or even that they know. For in the main knowledge about religions is acquired through inarticulate experience, on the one side, or through indoctrination, on the other. In both ways it is unreflective: the learner is dependent. The students think they know and understand things they do not know of their own knowledge. That is why they tend to assume they understand what we are saying. They assume they have already heard what in fact (in our minds) is fresh and unprecedented for them.

When we help students attain the clear capacity to distinguish new from old, the act of understanding from mere assent, the conscious deed of interpretation from the presumption of dumb familiarity, we lead them in mind through the very center of their existential task of growing up. I do not mean we make them less religious or more religious than they were, let alone better or worse Christians or Judaists. I mean we show them that there is more to be learned about what they think they already know, and that they can learn it. It is the experience of that kind of independence of intellect which will both prefigure and replicate the independence of personal existence each student has, in a brief time, to attain.

VII

Explaining why society and our community ought to know what we have to each comes at the end. Our own country has entered upon a period in its history much like that of the late adolescent, approaching the decisions of maturity. For a long time, like children, we pretended there was no world but our own. Then, in World War II and afterward, we pretended that the whole world was our own. Now is the time to come to terms with a world which is not our own, but in which we have a share. To recognize both what is ours and what is not ours is to understand what is foreign but what we can make our own.

It is this encounter with the alien which requires our community and society to take up the intellectual and cultural tasks of interpretation of what we do not understand out of the resources of what we deeply comprehend. This social and political task of making ourselves at one and whole with an alien world is something we cannot do, if we have not experienced the work in some small place. In the study of religions which are not ours we learn how to enter into worlds which belong to others.

That is why the importance of learning a foreign language and of learning about a religion other than our own is the same: it is to prepare us for the confrontation with difference, to educate our sympathies to welcome diversity, to discover what we can be in what we are not. We must learn to glory in the encounter with difference, not only because we have not got any choice. The reason is also that we should not want it otherwise. In finding out things we did not know, we learn. In encountering and entering into worlds we did not make, we discover. In the learning and discovery, we uncover in ourselves things we did not know were there. We find out we can be more than what we are.

The critical task facing this country in the world and in our life as a nation is to learn to confront difference. Our society now recognizes that there is no single normative culture for all of us to accept. Twenty percent of the population speaks Spanish. Nearly twelve percent is black. Three percent is Jewish. There is a growing minority of Moslems and Buddhists, both native and immigrant. I have the privilege of sitting on the National Council on the Humanities, governing body of the National Endowment for the Humanities, and so I always am studying proposals of many sorts, from many kinds of groups and organizations, in every part of the country. I marvel at the diversity. I am amazed that before us come the ideas of men and women who know how to find the humanist in all of us.

The world in which we live no longer concedes that one way of life or one system is valid for all. The world for which our students now prepare demands, therefore, the capacity to take two steps, first, to discover oneself in the other, so that the alien seems less strange, and second, to discover the other in oneself, so that the self seems more strange. When our students study the religion in which they were brought up and for the first time undertake the task of sympathetic, academic analysis and interpretation, they discover the alien in what they thought belongs to them. Questions which seem settled long ago turn out to be unsettling. The alien is within. Where we are most at home, there we are mostly strangers.

If our notion is that we study with profit only someone else's religion, we deprive ourselves of what we most require. To take one example, if contemporary Jews take for granted that they also know all about and define Judaism, they transform themselves from isolated and not necessarily representative or consequential facts about a given religion, Judaism, into the measure of all things Judaic. So they reduce a complex tradition, going back for nearly three millennia, into only its most current, and not demonstrably its most representative, form. The same is so for Christians. It is when our students realize that even what they think they know best, themselves and their own culture, contains mysteries yet to be uncovered that our work begins. It is when we understand that, in the work of learning, we remain perpetually outsiders in our own richly complex traditions, strangers where we feel most at home, that our work begins.

3. THE NEW SETTING FOR JEWISH LEARNING AND ITS CHALLENGES

The great movements in Judaism in modern times are the creation of intellectuals. Two dominant movements changed the face of the community and reshaped Jewish history: the development of non-Orthodox modes of Judaism, Reform in particular, and Zionism, the creation of Jewish nationality and the State of Israel. Both are the work, to begin with, of thinkers, not of doers, of scholars and intellectuals, rabbis and journalists, and above all, of university students. Reform is the work of scholars and students. Zionism is the creation of a journalist, Herzl, a novelist, Nordau, and Jewish students of that time, represented by Weizmann. For a long time thereafter Zionism was led by lawyers, judges, and other intellectuals.

This fact is important, because our present perspective is that Reform Judaism and Zionism depend upon the support of middle-class businessmen and of millionaire-politicians. We must not forget that the businessmen and politicians came aboard only much later. Zionism was already a safe investment. Reform Judaism was not created to serve as a vehicle for the bourgeoisie to legitimate their imitation of their neighbors' ways. Zionism was bitterly opposed by all of the Jewish millionaires whom Herzl approached. By the time the monied classes joined these movements, the movements themselves had ceased to serve as the generative force in the formation of values and ideals within the Jewish community. Indeed, they had passed from their creative stages entirely. They no longer found much that was new and interesting to contribute in the formation of the consciousness and imagination of Jewry at large. The two value-forming—mythopoeic—and vital, interesting movements in modern Judaism have passed into the hands of the middle class and rich businessmen. They exist chiefly to raise money so they may continue to exist.

If the creative forces in modern Jewry take shape on the campus, we must ask, what is the meaning of the newest university development, the academic study of the Jews and Judaism, broadly defined? The university is a quite new setting for Jewish learning. Its imperatives are only now becoming clear.

To begin with, we have to define the sort of university to which the field of Jewish learning responds. After all, many institutions of learning, not all of them of "higher learning," are called colleges or universities.

There are colleges of hair dressing and plumbing as well as of liberal arts learning. In as yet unpublished research Paul Ritterband has shown that Judaic studies find their original place in the research-oriented universities, only later on moving into the more serious liberal arts colleges, state and city universities and colleges, and the like. Accordingly, the university of which we speak is a place in which knowledge, its discovery, criticism, and transmission, takes the first place. Jewish learning is located within faculties devoted to serious study and serious teaching. It is not a subject much pursued at other sorts of colleges and universities.

With the increment of experience, the new generations of professors of Jewish studies learn about their new situation and its potentialities. The most important discovery is that the university is an essentially assimilatory agency. Differences of origin and culture are obscured. A single standard of thought, reason, and logic applies to all analysis and all data. There is no ethnic physics. Courses taught only by Jews, specifically for Jewish students, on the subject of Judaism are equally incongruous with the university setting. And above all, all statements of truth are subject to verification, therefore to the test of evidence and falsification.

The sociologist, Marshall Sklare, has already stated the assimilationist traits of universities so far as they affect the personal and social commitments of Jewish professors in general (*America's Jews* [N.Y., 1971], p. 68):

> The problem of maintaining a Jewish identity among academicians comes not so much from the possibility of a sudden rejection of that identity but rather from a diminished involvement in and commitment to the Jewish community. Gradually such commitment becomes less meaningful than commitment to one's profession and to the academic community. In the end commitment to the Jewish community may come to be replaced by commitment to the academic community, and to the value that the academic community places on universalism over particularism. . . .

Sklare illustrates his fine insight by reference to intermarriage among college students and professors.

But there is another point of relevance, the intellect. Let me now rephrase his observation: "The problem of maintaining Jewish studies as an ethnic field, validated entirely in terms of the prior ethnic affirmations of professors and students, comes not so much from the possibility of a sudden rejection of that approach but rather from a diminished involvement in and commitment to the social sources of its self-validation. Gradually Jewish studies as an ethnic field intended to strengthen the Jewish loyalty of the students and help them find meaning in being Jewish becomes less meaningful than commitment to the disciplines of the university's approaches to learning and to the values of the academic community. In the end commitment to the values of the Jewish community may come to be replaced by commitment to the values of the academic community, in particular to the value that the academic community places on universalism over particularism." I think the matter is clear and requires little elaboration.

To recapitulate the argument: The most vigorous and interesting things happening in Jewish life today are things which happen on the campus and in peoples' minds. The center of the Jewish learned world is now at least as much in secular universities as it is in Jewish institutions of Jewish learning. Considerably more scholars—that is, people working full-time at teaching and learning—are employed by universities than by Jewish seminaries, teachers' colleges, and the like. And the university is essentially an assimilatory agency, as Sklare says. Its values stress universalism over particularism. And the Jews are particular and inward-turning. The action in Jewish intellectual life—from which must come whatever vitality and vigor the Jews will have—has moved to the secular campus, and the secular campus lives by values which, on the face of it, are hostile to the conduct of Jewish intellectual life in its old ways.

To phrase the central question in simple terms: What are the models for university learning which are relevant to the Jews' situation as a particular people in a universal and open society? Having stated the question in these terms, I have of course phrased the central dilemma which has faced American Jews from the beginning. Just as we in universities are Jews in an undifferentiated and attractive world, so Jews in the open society of America have to find the measure of their lives in an undifferentiated and attractive society. What place for difference, with what justification, and above all, what is the meaning and what the end? Whatever theory we may develop to make sense of our situation in universities is apt to provide a theory for the situation of Jewry as a whole.

Let me now state the two contradictory theories of the place and shape of Judaic learning in universities.

The first holds that we do in the new home what we did in the old, but pretend to be doing something fresh. The second maintains that the task is integration and assimilation. The separationists seek to organize the field in autonomous departments of Jewish studies; the integrationists, primarily in disciplinary departments, perhaps joined through interdisciplinary committees or programs. The separationists identify themselves with ethnic studies, the integrationists do not. The theory of the separationists begins in the conviction that an entity, the "Jewish people," exists, not in faith but in fact, and that one therefore studies as a unity, and without regard to discipline, method, or inner, yet common, logic, the literature, history, and sociology of people in widely separated places and epochs. Jewish studies in an autonomous framework—whether yeshiva, seminary, or department of Jewish studies—measure their worth by their success in molding the values of the living generation. Jewish learning defined as Jewish studies is pursued not simply because it may illuminate some aspect of the humanities or social sciences, but because it will help the Jewish student to form beliefs by reference to the tradition of which he is part and should be part.

The contrary theory of the subject begins in the reassessment of assimilation, as phrased by Gerson D. Cohen ("The Blessing of Assimilation in Jewish History," in J. Neusner, ed., *Understanding Jewish Theology* [N.Y., 1973], pp. 251-58), "The first shibboleth which all of us have been raised on is that Jewish survival and above all Jewish vitality in the past derived in large measure from a tenacious adherence on the part of our ancestors to all basic external traditional forms." But this view is false, Cohen argues, and the facts in particular show it to be false. Cohen says, "There are two ways of meeting the problem of assimilation. The first is withdrawal and fossilization. . . . There is and always was an alternative approach of . . . utilizing . . . assimilation as channel to new sources of vitality . . . the healthy appropriation of new forms and ideas for the sake of our own growth and enrichment. . . . The great ages of Jewish creativity have always been products of the challenge of assimilation and of the response of leaders who were to a certain extent assimilated themselves. . . ." The theory of integration, further, holds that the Jewish data are to be subjected to the same methods and interpreted in accord with the same principles as pertain to all other data in the humanities and social sciences. There are no values and methods specific to the study of Jewry, distinctive to the analysis of Judaism in all its forms. The integrationist seeks to discern and understand structures, the separationist, to inhabit them. In the integrationists' view, commitment is to scholarly method and result and therefore to disciplinary department; in the separationists' view, commitment is to the content of what is studied. The former deems advocacy to relate to scholarly alternatives, not to the spiritual condition of students, let alone professors.

These conflicting theories of the field produce important curricular debates as well. Two major and contradictory theories presently guide the formation of programs in the field of Jewish learning in North America, Europe, and the State of Israel. The one denies the possibility of investigating matters of Jewish concern outside of specific disciplines. According to this theory, "Jewish studies" constitute a body of data subject to investigation in accord with various disciplines. Jewish studies are properly organized, within the curriculum, along disciplinary lines. They belong within departments defined by common methods. For example, one legitimate discipline, or rather, composite of methods, is that shaped within the academic study of religions. Accordingly, the disciplinary thinking emergent in the academic study of religions imposes its questions and its larger theoretical interests upon the formation of specific courses on Judaism as upon other religious traditions. There are, self-evidently, other valid and important disciplines pertinent to the study of the Jews, including Judaism. The work, however, is shaped within the conceptual framework of a departmental setting. It is to be guided by problems shaped by, and shared with, colleagues studying other data and from other perspectives.

The second theory, corresponding to the position of the separationists, is that Jewish studies should be organized where possible in a single department, without primary or fundamental regard to matters of method and discipline. The conceptions of method and discipline characteristic of this second position have not been spelled out. Rather, they are taken as self-evident, because the Jewish community outside the university and many Jewish scholars within it make the same assumptions about the Jews and their culture. And they also take the same position toward the university. The university is to be exploited for "Jewish survival." It enjoys no autonomy. It bears no legitimate character of its own. Yet the power of the separationist theory of Jewish learning is not to be dismissed because of the absence of intellectual articulation. On the contrary, much evidence of its compelling cogency is to be found in its present predominance. Large and powerful departments and institutes of Jewish studies exist. Seminaries, teachers' colleges, national associations of scholars, majors in Jewish studies, journals centering upon Jewish subjects with no interest whatever in disciplinary cogency—all of these testify to the weight and power of the non-disciplinary and essentially extra-university and even anti-university approach to Jewish learning, the approach which, as I said, stresses the self-validating, mythopoeic character of the data.

My hope is that I have presented the alternatives with a measure of respect for each. But now I must make explicit my implicit position on the issue. I believe that the goal of learning is to comprehend structures of knowledge, to apprehend how facts fit together and illuminate still larger sets of facts. I do not consider that knowing this and that about the Jews or about anything else constitutes the acquisition of significant knowledge. I find it self-evident that knowing about the Jews significantly and materially enhances our understanding of the humanities and humanity.

We have now to ask about the issue of objectivity, which is generally held to differentiate seminary from university studies in Judaism. It is widely supposed by separationists that the primary difference between universities and seminaries is that professors in universities are objective. But that is naive. They hold that university teachers do not advocate; they merely teach. In fact, professors in both settings perceive that facts bear meaning, constitute a whole which transcends the sum of the parts. They enter into ultimate engagement in what, to the world, is merely interesting. The commitment on both sides is the same. But the advocacy in form and objective is different on the campus. A university professor of Judaic studies does not advocate Judaism but ultimate seriousness about the problematic of Judaism, about the interpretation of Judaism as an aspect of the humanities, a very different thing. We are not agents of the Jewish community or rabbis. Our students have rights, after all, and one of these is the right to be left alone, to grow and mature in their own distinctive ways. They have the right to seek their own way, as we find ours, without being pestered. We are not missionaries, but professors. The professor leads, says, "Follow me," without looking backward to see whether anyone is there. The missionary pushes, imposes self upon other, autonomous selves. That is the opposite of teaching and bears no relevance to university scholarship. Our task indeed is to teach, which means, not to indoctrinate; to educate, never to train. There is a fine line to be found, an unmarked, but dangerously mined frontier, between great teaching and aggrandizing indoctrination. So there are risks to be endured in the search for the center and the whole. There are courtesies to be observed. The virtues of the professor are self-restraint and forbearance, tolerance and objectivity.

From one perspective, these virtues appear to begin in the conviction, held by the university professor and rejected by advocates of ethnic identification, that knowledge and understanding do not bring salvation. That is why, at a preliminary glance, they do not have to be imposed upon the other person. After all, if what I know will not cure what ails the other, why force it down his throat? Knowledge is not gnosis. It saves nothing. It cures nothing. It solves no problems, except by indirection. Knowledge is interesting and engaging, but serves itself. Separationists see the processes of learning as important because they serve a purpose beyond themselves, specifically, because they produce ethnic identification. They stem the tide of assimilation. They thus contribute to the solution of the contemporary "Jewish problem."

If knowledge—Jewish learning—is not asked to serve some other, extrinsic purpose, no one can seek salvation through learning. None can come to Jewish studies as a gnostic system and seek a gnostic experience of salvation. What salvation do we offer, who deem scholarship to be the recognition of ignorance, who seek consciousness not so much of what we know but of how we know and of what we do not know? Scholarship is drawn by self-criticism, compelled by doubt and curiosity. The professor knows the limits of knowing, exactly the opposite of the gnostic. Soteric gnosis is not ours to offer. What advocacy is there for skepticism and ignorance? How shall we advocate humility before the unknown, but arrogance to think we can know?

Yet that is not entirely fair to separationists nor wholly candid about the inner conviction of assimilationists. If we give our lives to what we do, then for ourselves we do find salvation. If what we give our lives to is learning, then learning for us bears soteric and salvific meaning. We cannot accuse the other side of caring and claim we do not care. That is not honest and does injustice to ourselves. We devote ourselves to the things we study, to our 'data. These data in their way take over and shape our consciousness. The things we study become part of ourselves. Whether or not this is deemed gnostic salvation is not quite to the point.

Let me propose a different distinction, a different set of alternatives for a theory of the university study of Judaism and the Jewish people. To begin with, let us call to mind the classic trilogy of Judaic theology, God, Torah, and Israel, meaning, the Jewish people. There was a time in which Jewish learning was undertaken in the service of God. The Jews today are secular. Whether in universities or in seminaries (excluding Orthodox yeshivot), they do not study for religious reasons. But in the contemporary Judaic consciousness, the element of Israel, the Jewish people, now stands at the fore. In what I have said, I hope with accuracy and fairness, about the professors who see themselves as contributing to the solution of the "Jewish problem," I find the focus upon that element. Accordingly, within the primary mythic structure by which Jews understand themselves, exactly that element—Jewish peoplehood—which predominates in the consciousness of the community at large also is central in the theory of advocates of survival through Jewish learning.

Yet there is a third element in the trilogy. It is that element which I think pertinent to the situation of university professors of Judaic studies: Torah, broadly understood as Jewish learning for its own sake. That element is remarkably congruent to the central value of university professors at large. Humility before the unknown and arrogance to undertake the task of learning, knowledge for its own sake—these are the shared and common values of our colleagues and ourselves. In physics or philosophy or engineering or religious studies or Judaic learning, we give ourselves to our data and are shaped by what we study. This, as I said, bears for us soteric and salvific meaning. I propose that element in the Judaic myth which, in its unfolding, best explains who we are and what we do, is Torah. *The seal of the Holy One, blessed be he, is truth.* In the nature of things to do our work in the university, we must assimilate, set aside parochial concerns and private realms of meaning in favor of the shared world of common discourse. The world of the university defines our lives together, and this accords, happily, with the definition imposed by Judaism upon those same lives.

The university is, as Sklare tells us, a place in which our commitment to the Jewish community is diminished, commitment to our profession and to the academic community and its values heightened. I argue exactly that: commitment to the Jewish community as we now know it *should* be replaced by commitment to the values of the academic community, so that, in time, the Jewish community will be reshaped by the values of learning, gain renewed access to its own intellect. Jewish studies in universities which do not lead to a shift in commitment and focus are unlikely to serve either the Jewish community or the university. But the value of the academic community is not principally emphasis upon universalism over particularism, though from Sklare's perspective (as from mine in Chapter 1) that is certainly the case. There are academic values which bear no relationship to the sociology of the academic community. I think the primary and dominant one is complete devotion to one's subject and the critical examination of the disciplines through which one investigates that subject. What subject do we study? To what data do we make that ultimate commitment of self and of mind? Self-evidently, we give our lives to learning about Judaism and Jews. We deem the act of knowing the Jewish sources to be its own validation. We deny it is to be justified by reference to anything beyond itself. We do not measure our success by whether our students go off and join Jewish organizations, refrain from eating pork, seek a Jewish mate, or do any of the other things which the Jewish community deems important. We do not even think that the rich student's mind is more important than the poor student's mind, and, in the context of the organized community, there can be no greater heresy than to deny the self-evident superiority of having money.

Such power as is ours is the power of our sources. What we have to offer is their beauty and the poetry of their logic. We are overcome by the ineluctable and ineffable force of this alien world, the reality constructed by our data. My own work for many years has been in the historical interpretation of the Judaic law, particularly the law dealing with purity. Now that law has not been kept, in the main, for nearly two millennia, and much of it is in any event imaginary and mythic. Yet as I plunge into its depths, I become intoxicated by its filigreed subtleties, its interplay of conception and formulation. The data, the facts of the law, take hold and begin to shape a new canopy, an arcane frame work of compelling meaning. I take as my task, therefore, to help others perceive the poetry of the law, framed as it is in its little, perfect units, spun out from generation to generation like a rope without end. If the law is seen to be mysterious and beautiful, in its form and in its substance, then, it is my conviction, it will capture others as it has taken my mind and my heart, and as it has engaged the intellects of so many, much greater learners, for a lifetime of centuries, eighteen hundred years, from the second to the twentieth.

At the beginning I pointed out that great events in the life of the Jewish people in modern times begin on the campus, among students and professors. They are carried forward by university graduates, journalists, lawyers, doctors, and other practicing intellectuals. Clearly, something very new and interesting begins to take shape in universities, an event, in Judaism, rich with potential force and complex meaning. Our theory of what happens on the campus, therefore, bears implications for what happens in the community. And that is so not solely for historical and sociological reasons, but also for practical ones. Today hundreds of full-time professors of Judaic studies, both of Jewish and of gentile origin, spend their lives in the humanistic study of Jewish texts, broadly construed.

If, as I have argued, these texts bear their own weight and power, they are bound to begin to reshape the imagination and even the character of the people who study them. These people, our students, go out into the community and help define it.

What then is the meaning to Jewry, therefore, of the renaissance of Jewish learning in universities? Within the tripartite structure of Judaism, God, Torah, and Israel, the second element once more comes to prominence, drawn to the fore in its remarkably just new context. For a century, the condition of the Jewish people, Israel, has occupied our minds. There has been no alternative. I need not rehearse our tragic history as a people. But in centering our attention upon our condition in the world, we have neglected our inner life, the rational construction of our minds and the revision of reality to respond to what is in our minds. We Jews do not perceive the world as Judaic tradition interprets it; nor do we see the world through other myth. Our tasks have scarcely allowed us to ask Judaic questions and seek Judaic answers, to interpret what happens in the context of the enduring perspectives of Torah. Indeed, the persistent tasks to be done for Israel, the Jewish people, have demanded otherwise. To survive in this world we have had to learn its ways and accept its disciplines. The world, alas, is our school. It imparts its meanings upon being Jewish, imposes upon us acute consciousness of "being Jewish" with little pity and no sympathy. Education in the Judaic imperatives takes place in the arenas of world opinion and in the headlines of newspapers. We have not enjoyed a moment of benign neglect, but an epoch of malignant attention.

But that has meant we could go on "being Jewish" by devoting our public selves to that aspect of our being. Our private lives, our inner reflections, our search and sense for individual meanings—these are unattended to. We are a generation of public commitment to Jewish affairs, and private neglect of the Jewish life. Devotion to Jewish activities and indifference to their inner meaning and direction share the same national soul. People who lavish their best energies, their money, and their time upon Jewish activities also live lives remote from distinctive and particular Judaic meanings. That is the result of the century we have endured, the unspeakable disaster, for Israel and Torah alike, of modern Jewish history. For the Jewish people in America and Canada, the opportunity has come to gain renewed access to the fundament of wisdom, the inner experience, of the Jewish people, even to transform the life of Israel through transcendent Torah.

For Torah too this unprecedented opportunity bears the potential of renewal. For if Jewry has found itself too busy for Torah, Torah also has been neglected, unable to speak and to be heard. Those who had access to its parts would say nothing of the whole. Even the parts they knew appeared to them distinct and separate, isolated both from one another and from the world of human affairs. They had no language, there were no words, neither could they make their voice heard. Torah existed, but not in, not for, this world. In anguished search for a place in the world, Israel joined the world, changed itself, its language, its clothing, its way of making a living, its conduct of life. Israel became part of the modern world not only in form, but in inner perspective. Torah, the most distinctive and particular aspect of the Judaic heritage, could do little but fall silent. Ours is the opportunity to speak out of the silence, for we do have some of the words, we do master the rudiments of the language, and our voice is heard. So far as we are taken up and reshaped by the power of the texts, ours is an authentic message, an insight of integrity.

But our voice is modulated by the shape of the hall in which it is heard. The words bounce against indifferent walls. We find ourselves in the lecture halls of universities, severe, undecorated places. Whether it derives from the austere heritage of our beloved New England, mother of the American mind, I do not know. But university classrooms and lecture halls, like New England churches, are strangely barren places, without art, without design, without color. Their light is unmodulated and pitiless. They are used for many subjects, so are meant to be neutral, hospitable to all but according special welcome to none. And, it goes without saying, their visual neutrality bears a deeper meaning. The world before us in universities is open, willing to listen, but only to one language for all. It is, as I have stressed, a world in which, in deep ways, people assimilate to common value and adopt a single culture, the discipline of mind. If there is diversity in the classroom, it is in clothing and cosmetics. It is not in special pleading. Accordingly, the world before us is curious about Jews and Judaism, but merely that. Our subject is no more and no less welcome than any other subject. We speak to issues common to all humanities and to humanity.

But, as I have argued, that is profoundly appropriate to the intellectual condition of contemporary Israel, the Jewish people. It too is neutral, open to, but unmarked by, Torah. Our existential circumstance within the university corresponds to that outside. The world flows through and beyond. Our students come from some place and go on to some other, and so do we, professors and Jews. What forms the Jewish problematic also is the issue of the common culture: the place of the particular in the undifferentiated world. Such theory as shapes the study of the Jews and Judaism in universities has at the end to interpret and respond to the condition of Jews and Judaism in the world outside universities. Within the disciplines and tasks of Judaic learning, we seek words that speak to all, but to none in particular, language to convey a distinctive perspective upon, and to, undifferentiated humanity. These words have then to address common concerns with uncommon truth.

Within Torah are such words, I think, because Jews who make Torah are human beings and part of a common humanity. Through the exceptionally particular language of Torah they give distinctive form to insight and truth deriving from experiences and perplexities common to the human condition. The Jews are a peculiar people, in their pilgrimage through nearly the whole of recorded history and across all the continents. But in their intense engagement with one another, with their peoplehood as Israel, they endure and record in Torah what happens to everyone and, at one time or another, everywhere. Their questions—the perplexities of life's course, the terror of holocaust and memory, the quest for redemption and for a house to have but not to come home to—these questions face the generality of humanity. Torah marks the human being as different, as Israel. But it does so by making Israel into humanity; Torah shapes the condition of Israel into a paradigm of the human condition. Torah is what makes the Jew into a *mensch*, "In our image, after our likeness." *So God created man in his own image, in the image of God he created him; male and female he created them.*

4. JUDAIC STUDIES IN UNIVERSITIES
Toward the Second Quarter-Century

The creation at Duke University of a new chair in Judaic Studies by the Smart Foundation presents the occasion for both celebration and reflection. We celebrate a munificent act of support for the newest expression of what is, in fact, a very old tradition of learning, that of studying about the Jewish people and Judaic religion. But recognition of the dimensions of such an endowment, the opportunity it represents, the challenge and the responsibility before us of the academy—that recognition demands much sober thought. Not only so, but we must ask ourselves what this chair represents in American and Canadian higher education. For the Smart professorship at Duke is one among many coming into being just now. I point to the List Professorship just now announced at Harvard University, the Koshland Chair at Stanford University, and numerous other endowed chairs as well. What happens at Duke, how people respond to the challenge and responsibility of the Smart Professorship, therefore defines a measure and makes a difference among the other great universities of the country, among which, here as in other ways, Duke University takes a leading position.

At some universities the creation of a named chair in Judaic Studies marks the beginning of a field. No tradition of learning, no experience of accumulated years of teaching and collegial scholarship, guides response to the opportunity of a chair. At other universities, symbolized by Duke University, a chair comes to bring final recognition to a field well-cultivated, an academic tradition richly and deeply expressed in years of effective teaching and important scholarship. Judaic Studies at Duke University, represented on the larger academic stage by Professors Eric M. Meyers and Kalman P. Bland, but also by Duke's undergraduate and graduate alumni, among whom I most cherish my own student, soon-to-be Professor Howard Eilberg-Schwartz of Indiana University, assuredly deserve the chair that comes today to the field at hand. So no one here needs the counsel and advice of an outsider, however well-meaning, such as myself. You have built on strong foundations. You today celebrate your completing a splendid edifice of education and scholarship.

Rather let me turn your attention to the larger setting in which today's event takes on meaning. For the proportions of the moment are grand.

With the creation of the Smart Professorship and similar endowed chairs at numerous distinguished universities, Judaic studies in American and Canadian universities move into a new age. One era ends, another begins. We stand upon the boundary. Mark the moment. What has changed? Let me characterize the shift in the character of the field by referring to my own career, just half over now. In 1960 I completed my Ph.D. and assumed my first academic position. At that time, nearly a quarter-century ago, one could count on one hand the endowed professorships in Judaic studies in universities. The entire number of positions would not take more than the other hand and not all of the ten toes. Today, as we all know, the field of Judaic studies has found a place in most departments of religious studies in the country; instruction in Hebrew, particularly modern Hebrew, is carried on in most departments of Near Eastern Studies. Some positions in history departments exist for various aspects of the history of the Jews, though the field of Jewish history has not established an academic presence of the dimensions attained by the fields of the study of Judaism as a religion, on the one side, and of the Hebrew language and literature on the other. Along these same lines, we find specialists in studies of the Jews and of Judaic learning in social science departments such as anthropology, sociology, and political science, in humanities departments such as philosophy and literature, as well as in history and religious studies. The principal disciplinary foci remain the academic study of religion, on the one side, and the study of Hebrew language and literature, on the other.

When, moreover, we take note of the exceptional growth in the number of positions in disciplinary departments, we must not miss a development of equal consequence. It is the formation of centers, programs, and departments of Judaic studies. In 1960 one could point only to Brandeis University, then as now a great center of strength in many aspects of Judaic Studies, and Yeshiva University. Today we see centers and programs at (for example only) Yale, Columbia, Harvard, and Brown, in the Ivy League, Wisconsin, Minnesota, Ohio State, and Indiana, in the Big Ten, Berkeley, in the great California system, and at many other places. (I hope and believe that in 1985 the first Department of Judaic Studies in the Ivy League will come into being at Brown University.) So the Smart Professorship marks the turning of the way. The quarter-century in which Judaic studies took shape has come to an end. A new age is upon us.

What are the two principal changes? First, in 1960 nearly all professors of Judaic studies were the sole representatives of the field in their own universities. Today, as we see at Duke and at the University of North Carolina, as at numerous distinguished universities, a critical mass of scholars comes into being, with three or five or even ten and more specialists on a single campus in various aspects of the study of the Jews and of Judaism.

Second, in 1960 majors or concentrations in Judaic Studies did not exist in many places outside of the two Jewish-sponsored universities, Yeshiva University and Brandeis, and only that at Brandeis had a distinctively academic character and purpose. Today, as is clear, Judaic Studies constitutes a recognized and broadly represented field of concentration or major.

So the problems of the period from the beginnings of the expansion of the field, in the late 1950s and early 1960s, and the problems confronting us today, do not correspond. Then we were alone, without a clear place, without a long tradition in our several universities, without a viable model for our courses or for our place in the curriculum. Nearly all of us in my age group found that we had to invent ourselves and our careers. We had to define for ourselves not only a profession, within the academic framework, but also an ethos and a definition of professionalism. In only a quarter of a century we have moved from primitive beginnings to a level of maturity and articulate, professional vision. There now is a tradition. There now is a definition. We know who we are and what tasks we have to do. We find in experience, in the record of failure but also success, both the lessons and the confidence to proceed to the next opportunities, the coming challenges.

What, then, are these opportunities and challenges? In a single word, we have to distinguish ourselves as a profession, within the academic world, and clearly to define what we do and what we do not do in that profession. Lines of structure and definition have now to reach clear demarcation. Beginning with the positive, what do we do? What, in our new age of large and well-articulated centers, programs, and departments, with our named chairs and our well-grounded careers, can we we do? And what must we do? Having asked so broad a range of questions, I immediately limit myself to three answers, recognizing the questions at hand deserve more extensive response that the occasion permits.

1. We are now not one or two isolated professors but five or ten, so we have to learn to work together.

2. Since we are now many in some one place, we have to learn to differentiate our work and attain a higher degree of specialization.

3. Since we propose to specialize, we have also to explain to ourselves and our students how our specializations come together to form a field of learning, a body of worthwhile knowledge.

Now that we are many, therefore, we have to think about ourselves differently and confront a new set of tasks. A member of a department knows how an individual's work fits into the larger composite of studies offered by the department. Such a person knows how to work in a cogent intellectual and educational framework with other members of the department. He or she knows the meaning of specialization and professionalization of learning, and aims at a vision of how the specialties fit together into a large and suggestive generalization. That (at least in theory and ideal) validates the organization of learning in universities today. So if we in Judaic studies now form large components of departments or autonomous centers, programs, or departments on our own, if, as I said, we now have colleagues in our area of learning whose work intersects with our own, if we now specialize in ways we could not before, if we now frame and define an academic specialization, a concentration or a major, in ways we did not—if the new age has come, what does it mean?

What we have to work out is how to work with other people, how to learn from them, how, in collaboration with others, to teach students who come to us, to teach in full knowledge that these same students study with others in our field, in our department, in our discipline. That is not a petty question, having to do merely with organizing a curriculum by assigning numbers to diverse courses. It is a question that points toward the center of the academic enterprise, so far as universities stand for the formation of cogent worlds of discourse. To state the task before us, we in Judaic Studies form a critical mass on many campuses so that we have to learn to talk with one another. To do so, we have to draw back from that unprofessional claim to know or have opinions on pretty much everything about everything, a claim characteristic of the days in which each of us was, in fact, the only specialist in Judaic studies on a given faculty. And, attaining a higher range of specialization, we have to confront afresh the issues of the interconnections of knowledge in the Judaic framework.

These general remarks demand at least one concrete example. If I specialize, as I do, in the study of the formative centuries of Judaism, in late antiquity, and if in the academic unit with me is a specialist in the study of the modernization of Judaic thought in the nineteenth and twentieth century, I have to explain to myself what I have to say to my colleague, and what he has to say to me. If he projects onto the age and kind of Judaism I study the issues of nineteenth century Judaic thought, he will not only commit anachronism. He also will not grasp what I am saying. If I take for granted he is doing what I do, "only" on later materials, I am guilty of the same obvious mistake. So what do we have to say to one another and to learn from one another? We do not posit the existence of a single, harmonious, and ubiquitous "Judaism," represented equally authentically by the things he studies and the things I study. So we have to find our way to one another step by step and rather slowly.

The route, of course, lies in discourse on those larger problems that we share: how to describe a system of thought? how to analyze the connections between that system of thought and those that come before and after? how to interpret the relationship between that system of thought and the social group that found in that system an encompassing explanation of its existence? When I grasp his points of inquiry, I learn not what the people he studies have in common with those I study. I learn, rather, another way to see things, perhaps a better way to unpack and analyze them, than I have on my own. Students who take both his course and my course learn different things from strikingly different minds. But they find themselves part of a common conversation. It is a shared and continuing inquiry into how people think things through within a common frame of reference. What strength to draw diverse people together inheres in a shared canon? In what way do Jews share a connected, even a continuous, human situation, and one that was and is distinctive to them?

This brief account of what I take to be principal intellectual challenges before us raises very concrete problems, demanding immediate attention. We can postpone issues of collegial and scholarly interchange. Many fields of learning attract loners. A narcissistic personality may find the university a perfect ambulatory sanitorium. But we cannot postpone issues of education. We make our living as teachers. Teaching young people is the most important thing any one of us does. The intellectual issues of cogency, connection, and continuity, to which I made reference just now, take concrete form in the curriculum, on the one side, and in text books, on the other. What we think as scholars reaches our students in our class room. The conduct of the class room depends upon the syllabus for our course, on the one side, and the setting of our course in the larger curriculum of our department, on the other. So education is the cutting edge of learning. Let me therefore speak of teaching, textbooks, and curriculum.

When we ask not about scholarship but about teaching, including the translation of scholarly results into terms accessible to students in the entryways of the field, things scarcely appear so hopeful. Let me borrow the words of a friend and close colleague to state my overall judgment of the problem and condition of academic Judaic Studies. Describing the American humanities in general, William J. Bennett, chairman of the U.S. National Endowment for the Humanities, states, "Humanities courses in colleges and schools have degenerated into a jumble of indiscriminate offerings, with no rationale and no guidance or coherence for the mind or imagination." He says, "Intellectual refinement and spiritual elevation are the traditional goals of the humanities and should remain so." Further, "The activities undertaken in the name of the humanities don't seem to add up to anything; they don't define anything. The studies we associate with the humanities today no longer stand for a unified set of principles or a coherent body of knowledge." The principal disciplines of the humanities, Bennett holds, "have become . . . fragmented, even shattered. . . . Humanities education is no longer an introduction to, and immersion in, the best thought and known. It is instead a collection of disconnected and often eccentric areas of inquiry. . . ."

If we simply substitute for "humanities in general" the words, "Judaic Studies in particular," we come up with an apt description of the present state of Judaic Studies viewed as an enterprise of public learning. I wish to spell this out with some care. The setting in universities requires professors to speak about things anyone can learn, in ways anyone can master, about facts and truths relevant to anyone's nurture in humanistic learning. So people in the academy engage in public learning, in completely accessible discourse. Indeed, to make the Jews' particular learning general, to show the general in the particular, to allow to outsiders access to what is private and shows its public side—these constitute the perpetual educational challenges to the humanities, as to all modes of creativity.

Teachers of Jewish studies have the task of contributing interesting specific examples—learned in all their specificity—to a common inquiry, to exemplify shared concerns, to speak to a single agenda, and to talk a language of universal reference. To do these things, they have to work out of a well-crafted program of learning. They must be able to describe the field and to explain it to whom it may concern, to whom it ought to prove interesting. These are not outlandish expectations. They confront every field. Bennett asks that activities add up to something, define something: stand for a coherent body of knowledge. Judaic Studies *are*—they are things one might know. But one cannot use the verb iist after the subject, "Judaic Studies." Why not? Because Judaic Studies is not yet a coherent body of knowledge.

Let us turn to two specific aspects of Judaic Studies in the academic sector of Jewish learning and point to educational problems at hand. Both concern the way in which Jewish learning in the academy takes shape as a set of coherent pieces of knowledge and how those who give the field shape join together and try to teach each other. They are (1) curriculum and (2) the literature of textbooks.

Why are these important? The reason is simple. The future of Judaic Studies as an academic discipline in the USA and Canada will be decided by the state of Judaic Studies within the university curriculum. (Neither seminaries nor Israeli universities will make much difference in the future, as they do not now.) If people in general think Jewish Studies have something worthwhile to teach, they will want to study that subject. They will encourage students to take courses. Scholars of Jewish Studies will take a critical part in the common intellectual life of the university. If Jewish scholars of Jewish Studies think they have nothing to say that anyone not "like us"—not "Jews of our very particular definition"—would want to know, Jewish Studies will pass from the scene. The successors will trudge back to the ethnic and parochial settings of learning from which the bulk of today's academic practitioners of Jewish learning without regret have taken leave.

Let us then speak of textbooks. Textbooks scarcely exist in yeshivas and seminaries. The world of classical Jewish learning, unlike the academic setting, produces no model. Why no textbooks in yeshivas? By definition, the textbook is the holy text the student studies. The conception that teachers have to bring into existence well-crafted and thoughtful books, to explain a subject or a document step by step and stage by stage, proves alien. Why so? Because there is one teacher, Moses, our rabbi. He has so laid out the Torah as to provide Israel with all the textbooks it can ever require. When we turn to the diverse disciplines in which Jewish learning takes place, we find ourselves not far from the same world-view.

First, where there are textbooks at all, they constitute little more than "collections of texts," not reasoned accounts of a subject, laid forth in well-crafted sequence. Anthologies of texts do not constitute textbooks. But for a considerable part of the textbook literature, that is all there is. Second, for a great many specific fields, there are not even anthologies. One who plans to construct a course in the history of the Jewish people in modern times in Europe will look in vain for anything written with the college student in mind. Beyond rather out-dated and wooden accounts, written to display information, not to raise and solve problems or argue theses or conduct systematic analyses, there is nothing. And in that area we deal with a popular subject. How matters turn out in the less commonly-taught subjects scarcely requires review.

We turn then to the curriculum. A curriculum tells not merely what subjects are taught. It constitutes a judgment upon culture in its intellectual form, that is, the organization of a field, a statement of what is important, an assessment of what forms that body of worthwhile knowledge that a student masters. In the classical settings of Jewish learning, the curriculum came down from Heaven: Bible, Talmud, associated rabbinical writings. Knowing these things self-evidently mattered. Within the documents, moreover, everybody knew how to choose the more important from the less important. A common consensus governed what people studied first, what they learned only later on. In the modernized Jewish schools, furthermore, the received curriculum of Jewish learning both found replication and enjoyed augmentation. In addition to the established texts and subjects, others take their turn as well. Bible and Talmud, studied in old and also new ways, now make room for Hebrew literature, or Jewish history, or other subjects, mostly of a neo-classical order. For all of them, the value of knowing things remains self-evident: defined by the social setting and institutional context. The shape, structure, value of the curriculum require little articulate exposition. In Jewish schools everybody knows what you do, in what order, for what purpose, and with what result, on earth for the sake of blood and peoplehood for the modernized schools, in Heaven for the received ones. In this regard the curricula of the Jewish seminaries contrast favorably with those of the diverse universities. Indeed, one can make sense of why, in a rabbinical school, students study one subject rather than some other, or one more than another. But in universities we cannot discern patterns of courses, so it is not possible even to describe and explain how and why, beyond the elementary course in Hebrew language, one thing comes before or after some other.

If, in the academic world, professors of Jewish Studies follow well-constructed curricula, they have not said so in generally accessible publications. Students going from one school to another (as they do) discover no relationship whatever between what they have learned and what they are going to learn. Whether we turn to the disciplinary fields of history, involving Jewish history, or literature, involving Hebrew literature, or the study of ancient Near Eastern civilization, involving old Jewish texts, we find no theory that might encompass the diversity of course-sequences. True, in religious studies we do. But it is only because the field is new and small. Practitioners of the religious study of Judaism come from a handful of graduate programs that exhibit a shared and articulated program of inquiry. But even here the program is rhetorical, not practical. Further, while some few textbooks are widely used and go through edition after edition, beyond the elementary level we see in the academic study of Judaism as a religion no more coherence, no more evidence of a well-constructed curriculum in common, than we do in the other disciplinary areas.

And in saying this, I refer only to the disciplinary departments—history, literature, religious studies—in which Judaic Studies take their place alongside other topics. What shall we say about the non-disciplinary and anti-disciplinary departments, centers, programs, majors, minors and concentrations, in Jewish studies? Such words as "chaotic" and "incoherent" suffice to say what is going on, which is nothing in particular: there is no curriculum.

Curriculum and textbooks go together. If professors know precisely what they want to teach, they also can construct textbooks for teaching it. But if not, then textbooks will prove aimless and useless. The point of differentiation rests upon a single issue: do professors have points they wish to make? Or are they presenting more information? If they construct their curriculum as an argument, or if they aim to conduct a coherent inquiry into a set of problems, then courses will relate to one another, and, course by course, students will gain not merely information but understanding. Facts will cohere and form statements, intelligible propositions, judgments of the way things are in general.

The difference between the academic world and the conduct of Jewish learning in Jewish circumstances is simple. That context that imparts and imposes definition derives, for Jewish-sponsored Jewish learning, from the Jewish situation itself. Being Jewish by itself defines that curriculum. Everyone in the classroom of a synagogue or *yeshiva* knows precisely why each bit of information is important and must find its place in the student's memory and mind. The data constitute a given (so to speak). The facts must be known because they must be known. Why? Because to be a Jew, these are things you have to know. It is a powerful rationale for a curriculum and an education, and it works, as indeed it should. Existence frames the curriculum.

But when that rationale proves simply irrelevant, as it does in universities, what takes its place? That is to say, professors have to frame an equally decisive thesis of why they teach one thing and not some other, of what imparts importance to facts, and of why one sentence—one book, one entire course—coheres with the next to form a statement of substance and of meaning. In the university "being Jewish all together," the apologetics of blood and peoplehood, no longer marks the limits of discourse or imparts meaning to whatever falls within those limits. Then other social data, facts to account for why people do what they do, together, in just this way, in just this place, must make their impact. That apologetics serves Israeli educators, not only at the university level, as much as it does American Jewish schools. It hardly fits into the university classroom, because not all the students and professors derive from Jewish parents or regard themselves as Jewish. The same social and cultural pluralism characteristic of university studies at large also defines the circumstance for Judaic studies. That fact makes all the difference.

The simple fact is that in universities, studies do pursue a common program of inquiry. Professors seek to carry out a single, fairly cogent, task of learning and understanding. It is no longer faith seeking understanding through information, as in the Jewish sector of Jewish learning. The humanistic and social scientific agenda define the search of learning: search for interesting examples for analysis, important and suggestive cases for detailed testing of generally-useful propositions. Above all, when humanists and social scientists study some one thing, they seek evidences of what is general to many things, examples of some fundamental issue in the human condition. As Jonathan Z. Smith states in connection with the academic study of religion:

> The student of religion must be able to articulate clearly what "this" rather than "that" was chosen as an exemplum. His primary skill is concentrated in this choice. This effort at articulate choice is all the more difficult, and hence all the more necessary. . . . Implicit in this effort at articulate choice are three conditions. First, that the exemplum has been well and fully understood. This requires a mastery of both the relevant primary material and the history and tradition of its interpretation. Second, that the exemplum be displayed in the service of some important theory, some paradigm, some fundamental question, some central element in the academic imagination of religion. Third, that there be some method for explicitly

relating the exemplum to the theory, paradigm, or question, and
some method for evaluating each in terms of the other.

Smith's thesis concerning the definition and program of the academic
study of religion pertains to all academic work, whether social scientific
or humanistic.

In universities learning of facts is essential but insufficient, just as is
the case in the setting of Jewish learning for Jewish purposes. In that
other setting, what next is demanded is the doing—the performance of
deeds of faith or nationality. In the academic sector what then is
demanded? It is the making of connections, the moving from the specific
and particular to the general and broadly consequential. But the same
issue confronts all curricula, hence all textbooks: So what? In the Jewish
sector of Jewish learning, we may readily identify a number of answers
to the question, So what? But in the academic sector of Judaic Studies,
such answers do demand articulation. That is to say, If I know this fact,
what else do I know on that account?

To state the present condition of curricula and therefore also textbooks, scholars of Judaic Studies have yet to meet that demand. Outside
of the beginning stages of the study of the Hebrew language, I cannot
point to a well-examined theory of how a course should take shape or
where a course finds its place within a large set of courses, a major, a
concentration. In yeshivas everyone knows what he is doing and why. In
seminaries people tend to know what they are doing and why. How so?
The momentum of the program of the nineteenth century "science of
Judaism," *Wissenschaft des Judenthums*, has not wholly run out. Conse-
quently, even in some university settings in America, many in Europe,
and all in the State of Israel, a great many people take for granted they
know exactly what they are doing and why, even if they cannot say so.
The reason is that they do not consider they have to say so: "We all
know. . . ."

Of course, if scholars cannot say what they know, they scarcely
know it. And, more to the point, if they cannot defend what they know
from criticism, what they think they know hardly is worth knowing. I do
not mean to suggest that the classroom in Judaic Studies in universities
shelters only purposeless blather, a mere babbling of disconnected facts,
a trivial caricature of antiquarian collecting. People study more than the
ethnography of gathering and hunting. Nor do I mean to propose that
one curriculum would serve all settings. Absence of general consensus
about questions of curricula does not signify deep demoralization among
the practitioners of Judaic Studies in academic contexts. I mean only to
suggest that the abysmal condition of the textbook literature, on the one
side, and the absence of sustained public discourse about questions of
curriculum—the major or concentration, the organization of the subject

for our students and ourselves—hardly justify confidence. The unprecedented setting by no means promises an important educational and cultural future.

Let me state very briefly how my colleagues and I have proposed to construct at Brown a cogent curriculum for our undergraduates. To state matters very simply, we give disciplinary courses in an interdisciplinary concentration. The Program serves as an interdisciplinary focus for studies of Jews and Judaism, including, but not limited to, historical, linguistic and philosophical perspectives and approaches. The chronological scope of the program's area of interest includes ancient Israel as well as modern Jews and modern Israel. Represented within the faculty associated with the Program in Judaic Studies are three principal humanistic disciplines: history, literature, and religion. Work in the social sciences—sociology and political science—is carried on as well. The undergraduate curriculum of the Program's courses is organized along *disciplinary* lines. The undergraduate concentration of the Program, for its part, is developed along *interdisciplinary* lines. It follows that the Program in Judaic Studies is not a non-disciplinary exercise in Jewish studies, but at every point a carefully crafted effort to show how diverse academic disciplines deal with a single subject, the Jews. The educational goal of the concentration is to provide students with a clear idea of how different approaches to the framing and answering of questions of systematic learning deal with the same social entity over a long period of history. Studying the Jews' history, the history of their religion, their languages, their diverse literatures, as well as the sociology, politics and philosophy characteristic of their community, the student learns three important things: first, at least some of the facts of the matter, that is, some Hebrew, some knowledge of history, some mastery of the description, analysis and interpretation of the religion of the Jews; second, at least some clear knowledge of how a historian, a sociologist, a political scientist, a philosopher, or a scholar of the history of religions frames questions and answers them; third a preliminary notion of what it means to look at the same thing from different angles.

In alluding briefly to the way in which my colleagues and I have thought through the matter of a cogent curriculum for Judaic studies, I mean to make only one point. Once we in Judaic Studies become more than a handful, we have to face a new and interesting set of questions. These questions define the intellectual tasks of the next quarter-century. We enter the age in which, with named chairs and fully articulated centers, programs, and even departments, Judaic Studies reaches maturity as a substantial presence in American academic learning.

Let me close with specific reference once again to Duke University, though the message needs to be heard elsewhere. Because the earliest positions in Judaic Studies developed in departments of religious studies and departments of Near Eastern languages and literatures, people have tended to think of Judaic Studies as a subdivision of either the study of religion or the teaching of languages (or both). True enough, one discipline critical to the nurture of Judaic Studies within the humanities indeed is the academic study of religion. But the subject at hand presents interesting problems of learning and research to all humanistic and social scientific disciplines capable of illuminating the inner life of humanity and of humanity in community. The Jews have produced diverse histories and cultures. These always have formed an aspect of the context in which Jews lived. They always, in addition, have stood in relationship to, in tension with, the continuity of the Jewish people. These diverse histories and cultures, languages and literatures, societies and even economic and political entities derive their vitality from the diverse forms and versions of Judaic religious systems. But no one imagines that history is exhausted by the study of religion. No one supposes that literature is solely a problem in the description and analysis of religion. Nor can social scientific inquiry stop at the frontiers of the inner life of the Jewish people.

To be sure, it is quite natural to regard the Jews as a religious group. But the Jews, while a religious group, are not a religious group in the way in which the Methodists or the Baptists are a religious group, nor in the way in which the Roman Catholics are, nor are they a nation-religion either, in the way in which the Armenians are. Jews have traits in common with these diverse groups. But the histories and cultures and societies and economic and political entities that, through time and through change, Jews have created for themselves present data at least as worth systematic attention as the Judaisms that Jews have made for themselves. Here at Duke, where the study of religion enjoys so formidable a presence, in the setting of a great divinity school and graduate faculty in religion, it is entirely proper for a principal emphasis to focus upon Judaism as a religion. But it would not serve learning to limit to one important aspect what we may wish to know about the subject at hand. The disciplinary diversity of what you do at Duke will present an influential model to us all.

5. TOWARD THE DISCIPLINARY EXPANSION
OF JUDAIC STUDIES

The state of Judaic studies reveals itself only through the professional standards of the professors in the field. The iron law of learning stands firm: you are what you do. Solid achievement in the end disposes of claims to standing and reputation. In stating matter in this way, I simply apply to the field at hand exactly those standards that apply to all other fields in the academic setting. Solid achievement does matter. Contributions to learning do register and even bring honor. The approbation of the elders, the recognition of cliques and claques, the approval of the theologians and guardians of the faith, the recognition of the keepers of the grail—none of this counts in the end. Why not? Because academic learning is secular. Honor is achieved, not conferred. Academic learning is public and uniformly accessible to all. Academic learning is open to rational discourse. The university ultimately, if not immediately and not always, demands that canons of reasoned and even civil discourse apply. *Odium theologicum* may dispose of claims to theological truth. *Odium scholasticum* ultimately will not settle issues of learned inquiry. In so stating, I express not personal faith but iron facts of academic life.

Now when we take up the standing of Judaic studies in the academic setting, we observe a strange conflict, one that alerts us to an interesting problem in the realm of learning.

On the one side, Judaic studies continue nearly unabated an expansion that got underway in the early 1960s. Marks of the latest increase in the representation of the field derive from the creation of endowed chairs in numerous universities as well as in the increase in the number of positions in a given university from one to two to four and still more. Accordingly, from the vigorous increase in the number and standing of positions in the field, we should guess that Judaic studies has attained a remarkable level of achievement. We should assume two things. First, important contributions to learning do emerge. Second, the field has attracted the interest of colleagues in other fields, because the methods and theories emergent in researches in the field at hand turn out to stimulate the mind and imagination of colleagues in other fields. So we should anticipate that in the field of Judaic studies in this country, important books now open up new areas of inquiry, and suggestive and challenging books presently expose methods and theories of research useful to many areas of inquiry. By a strictly academic criterion, these two traits ought to characterize a field of learning subject to the massive expansion in academic representation characteristic of Judaic studies for nearly twenty-five years. So much for expectations.

But the curious conflict comes when we ask about the concrete attainments of scholars who gain the new positions, particularly the endowed ones, in the more prestigious universities. We have the right to ask whether the newcomers to academic honor in the form of named chairs equal in solid accomplishment the holders of named chairs in other fields in their own universities. No one has the right, after all, to insist that, to make one's way in Judaic studies in a university, a person must reach a higher level of solid achievement than others in the same university. But we have every right to ask whether professors in named chairs in prestigious universities may point to books of the quality and number of those of colleagues in the same departments and universities. And while number may seem a petty consideration, in fact sociologists of learning do insist that quantity forms a measure of quality. They have shown that people who publish a lot commonly have a great deal to say to their colleagues, and people who do not publish a lot also gain slight attention for the little that they do publish. So while quantity is not the same thing as quality, quantity does help measure excellence. That having been said, we turn to the holders of the leading chairs in Judaic studies and discover that in the main, though not invariably, those scholars may list, as their scholarly publications, only their dissertations. In some instances, they have published a second scholarly book. In many, they have not. Looking at the Ivy League, for instance, we find a fair amount of editing of books, popular books, conferences, published lectures, and the like—not a lot, but some. But when we ask, "Exactly what books have you published as *sustained* contributions to learning," in most cases the answer in simple: "My dissertation. But I'm working on. . . ." In a few cases the answer is, "My dissertation and one other book." Since Ivy League and equivalent universities simply are not one-book faculties, the picture is clear. The standards of solid achievement characteristic of prestigious faculties do not apply to Judaic studies. What that means is that other than academic standards do apply.

Accordingly, we return to the strange conflict to which I referred. Judaic studies have vastly expanded in the number and quality of professorships. But Judaic studies have not met those standards of solid achievement that apply to other fields, old and new, in the universities in which they locate themselves. With important exceptions we have to conclude that Judaic studies do not constitute much of a scholarly ornament to the universities in which they are pursued. In particular the scholarly standing and achievement of those universities do not characterize the field of Judaic studies in those same universities. The reason, I would suppose, is that the people who make appointments in the field do not demand the same achievement, on the one side, and the people who make recommendations for appointment invoke criteria other than the usual ones, on the other. The approbation of the elders, the approval of cliques and claques, even theological approval and the benediction of the guardians of the faith and the keepers of the grail do matter. These things matter a lot.

Now in reporting the curious conflict between the growth of the field and the mediocrity that characterizes the expanding field, I do not mean merely to ask people to wring their hands. If universities took the field of Judaic studies seriously, the remarkably limited achievements requisite for distinguished appointment would likewise no longer suffice. Universities after all do make appointments in response to considerations other than of scholarly achievement, capacity to teach, intellectual leadership. They are as interested in the feelings of those presently on the scene as in the promise of those coming to join the community. The mediocre standing of the generality of scholars in Judaic studies derives not from the promise of the field of Judaic learning but the indifference of the faculties, by definition in other areas, who have borne responsibility for making appointments in Judaic studies.

That is to say, when a faculty makes an appointment in a field not represented in its midst, that faculty makes a judgment upon itself and its own standards. If the professors in a given department take their own work seriously, they will look for people at least as accomplished as themselves. Some professors will seek colleagues still more accomplished than they are, persons from whom they can learn things they do not know. The definitive mark of the ambition for scholarly greatness, after all, is the humility to learn from others. The faculty member who engages in ongoing programs of research will demand of new colleagues, "What can you teach me? How can you make life here still more stimulating than it already is?" Those who have done little by definition cannot answer those questions in a persuasive way. Those who engage in their own quest will listen eagerly to questions of others and will pose inquiries to others. That is the way of learning—the only way.

So the mediocrity of Judaic studies testifies to the character of the disciplines and departments in which Judaic studies have taken root. What we learn about the modest expectations of solid achievement characteristic of holders of named chairs in the field is not about those professors or even that field. What we learn is that the departments that made those appointments either do not care much about the field (and so accept as a given its total politicization and its reduction to matters of personalities), or themselves do not maintain higher standards.

Let us proceed to ask ourselves what sorts of departments have served as principal hosts for the expanding field of Judaic studies. These are three: departments of religious studies, departments of Near Eastern studies (or other language departments), and departments of Judaic studies—in roughly that order of importance.

Departments of Judaic studies rapidly lose attention in that amorphous form in which they have flourished, because they put together everything with everything else. They by definition have lacked all disciplinary definition. Everyone has an opinion on everything. In all, the non-disciplinary departments or centers or programs persist in a tradition of generalism in an academy that has long since come to recognize the priority of specialization. So we cannot have expected more from that sort of department than we do from any other department of the same classification, that is, any other non-disciplinary department.

What we learn about departments of Near Eastern studies and their equivalents is that departments devoted mainly to the study of languages and texts have lost such intellectual vigor as they had in their initial stages in the last century. We need not enter into the interesting debates, for example, about the value of Oriental studies (in their Near Eastern mode) to concede that those departments, as well as their national organizations and publications, so far as they remain in the humanities narrowly construed as philology, practice a sophisticated form of hunting and gathering. When the scholars get together, they play show and tell and (if they have conscience at all) call the result ethnography or philology. So why expect much of Judaic studies in the setting of Near Eastern studies (excluding the social scientific, including the historical, aspect of Near Eastern studies)? As I said, Judaic studies cannot prove themselves more vigorous, more interesting, than the other subjects with which they are associated in a common discipline. The intellectually arid character of the generality of Near Eastern studies (again, except in their social scientific modes) obviously explains, also, the vapid traits of Judaic studies practiced in the same setting.

And that brings us to religious studies. Let me say flatly that no field in my view enjoys a more promising future or a more disappointing present than the academic study of religion. Why so splendid a future? Because the subject forms the center of civilization, engages our attention whenever we reflect on what it means to be what we are, political animals. We cannot hope to understand humanity, past or present, without an ongoing engagement with that protean force that integrates and makes whole both the inner being and the social life of humanity, I mean, religion.

But why the disappointing present? Because, among all disciplines in the humanities today, I find it difficult to locate one so lacking as religious studies in a clear program of inquiry, on the one side, and a well-composed set of criteria of knowing good from bad, on the other. Because the consensus that defines the disciplines of the academic study of religion proves fragile, departments of religious studies make a place for astoundingly diverse inquiries. Professors who ordinarily belong in history departments work alongside professors who commonly belong in divinity schools (whether Judaic or Protestant or Roman Catholic). Professors who do what sociologists or anthropologists do work alongside professors who do what philosophers do. Now that disciplinary diversity can prove a source of intellectual vitality, as people talk with one another and learn from one another's questions and answers. But in so fragile a field as the one at hand, diversity turns out to mask chaos. Out of fear of reading anyone out of the field altogether, people tolerate as the study of religion anything that, in some way or another, makes reference to whatever anyone can call religious, from psychoanalysis to socialism. Accordingly, philologians work in departments of religious studies, so long as, on occasion, they work on texts deemed religious. Lay psychoanalysts call themselves professors but care for souls as if they were chaplains. Historians work in departments of religious studies, on the condition that, on occasion, they pay some attention to a group regarded in some way or another as religious. Lacking a vital center, members of departments coexist without collegiality of an intellectual character.

Why, then, should we express surprise that, in so weak and intellectually limited a setting as the academic study of religion, Judaic studies should make their way, as they in fact have made their way, pretty much on their own terms. And these terms, it is clear, are still defined mainly by outsiders to the field of the study of religion, indeed, outsiders to the academy altogether. How so? The standards in the main are set by the dictation of those elders, those cliques and claques, those politician-theologians, those guardians of the faith, those keepers of the grail, who have at heart an interest in something other than solid academic achievement. So politics, personalities, and power dominate. What people actually do is subject to systematic denigration, while those who do things at all find themselves the object of campaigns of demonization and character assassination. Since for twenty-five years my work has been boycotted and vilified, often on the basis of comically trivial errors (readily corrected, of course), I know whereof I speak. In a field in which books simply do not get reviewed at all, and in which people who have written no books beyond the dissertation gain named chairs, the state of affairs is entirely clear.

What is to be done for Judaic studies (and, by the way, for religious studies in those places in which the discipline of religious studies languishes)? I see two choices.

Either the academic world has now to declare in bankruptcy the field of Judaic studies (and the discipline of religious studies).

Or the academic world has to take over and make its own the field of Judaic studies (and the discipline of religious studies).

Matters cannot, and will not, go on as they are, because the stench of the scandal of mediocrity and lassitude has reached beyond the circles that have long been privy to it. People in high places in the national learned societies, in the Federal government and in the foundations, even in the world of Jewish philanthropy which has come up with vast sums for endowed chairs, all know that many of the emperors are naked. Because matters have now become public, the academic public does know, does recognize, exactly what for a quarter-century has happened in Judaic studies in universities—and what, also, has yet to take place. How so?

A field has made its entry on terms other than academic ones. A field has brought to the academy standards and modes of behavior and public discourse that do not belong. The limits of condescension, permitting people to tolerate in a despised minority what they would not accept in themselves, therefore have now been reached.

The reason that Judaic studies ought not to enter bankruptcy requires only routine, casual statement. The subject-matter is too suggestive, too important. The academic constituency in diverse fields of learning is too substantial, too much interested. Altogether too much is at stake for learning, for education in the deepest sense, for the academic world to cast adrift a cargo so rich as the one at hand, merely because the ship is infested by rats. The promise of the field of Judaic studies for the broadest ranges of inquiry into human behavior in society, in the social sciences, as well as the human imagination and intellect, in the humanities—that promise can yet be kept. The Jews as a group, the systems of thought and the ways of life that constitute the species of the genus, Judaism—these will make their remarkable contribution to the study of society and humanity, as much as, from nearly the beginning of recorded history to our own day, the Jews have made theirs: not enormous, but interesting, not paramount, but suggestive.

What is to be done? Where we are weak, there we discover how we may become strong. Judaic studies constitute a field, serving a multitude of disciplines. Then let the remedy derive from the disciplines of the academy, with each discipline asked to make its own those data deriving from Judaic studies that prove relevant to its broader inquiry. What is wrong with a field lacking all standards? It is a simple fact. Standards emerge not from fields of learning (area-studies) but from disciplines. Then let the disciplines take over the field and, as I said, make that field over into raw materials for the several disciplines of learning. Disciplines define the questions we propose to address to any area of learning. Disciplines explain the ways in which we find answers to our questions. Disciplines dictate how we know where we may be wrong and how we may validate our proposals. Accordingly, we turn to the disciplines of social scientific and humanistic learning and ask them to take over the data deriving from yet another area of information, the Judaic one.

Now, one may fairly argue, the discipline of religious studies has had twenty-five years in which to show what a discipline may do in the transformation of a field of learning. By my own word, religious studies has imposed on Judaic studies no solid measure of achievement and defined no public standard of success. The reason is that that field has proved broad but shallow, widely represented, but representative of the mediocrity of humanistic learning that, all in all, characterizes the quarter-century of growth of the academic study of religion now coming to an end. I remain hopeful for the academic study of religion, even though, in my own university, the field has little in which to take pride. Why do I remain committed to the academic study of religion? It is because the study of religion defines one of the great intellectual adventures of the academy to come.

At the same time, I seek the reform of Judaic studies in another place altogether. It is in the entire range of the disciplines of the social sciences and the humanities. What I mean to say is that, with the expansion of the several humanistic and social science disciplines into the area of Judaic studies, the field of Judaic studies will undergo that transformation that will turn the field into a productive locus of learning. When historians, sociologists, political scientists, as much as scholars of literature, art, philosophy, linguistics, and also the study of religion, take over the field at hand, then the standards generally prevailing in history, sociology, political science, literature, philosophy, and also the academic study of religion will apply.

Then, but only then, the area of Judaic studies will attain naturalization within the academic world. And at that time, and only under those circumstances, the professional standards of the university professors overall will dictate and differentiate here, as they do everywhere. Solid achievement then can matter, also, in Judaic studies, and civil discourse then can characterize scholarly conversation, also, in Judaic studies.

I do not mean to blame the failures of my own field on others. But I do claim that universities have tolerated in my field mediocrity and amateurism that they do not accept in other fields. So I do demand that condescension bordering on contempt give way to an attitude of respect and expectation. Only when universities tear down the walls of that intellectual ghetto, built by Jews and tolerated by others, walls protecting Judaic studies as practiced by insiders for insiders, will Judaic studies gain that academic citizenship, that passport to rigorous learning and participation in public debate, that marks authentic life in the realm of learning.

Part Three

SCHOLARSHIP AND POLITICS

6. THE CRISIS OF JEWISH LEARNING IN AMERICA

I

The field of Jewish studies in American colleges and universities is in flux. There is no consensus on fundamental issues of education and curriculum, scholarship and method, little agreement, for instance, about what should be taught, the disciplinary auspices (if any) under which the field should develop, the critical issues for discussion, foci and tools of research. It is also in flux in another respect. "Jewish studies" is a field in which amateurs find their way in and out, in which people do not yet perceive the subject as worthy of sustained and professional concern. Debates persist, for instance, upon objectivity, as if we knew that about which we are supposed to be objective. In many, though not in all, areas of Jewish learning, moreover, we find a mode of critical discourse familiar from the world of *yeshivot*, and described by Rabbi Oscar Fasman ("Trends in the American Yeshivah Today," *Tradition* 9, 3, 1967, p. 60), as follows: "Particularly prevalent among *yeshivah* students between the ages of sixteen and thirty, [the term *bittul*] is reflected in phrase, expression, and gesture to indicate that people not of our type are unworthy of quotation, or even of mention. Why listen to anything such people say, why observe anything they do, why be interested in their experiences? Because the human mind cannot cage viewpoints once embraced, the philosophy of *bittul* never ends, however, with this derisive sneering at only those far out of the circle. And often a Torah student is deeply wounded by the discovery that his method of interpreting a complex paragraph in the Code of Maimonides is brushed aside without any reverence by scholars of another school. A wise observer once remarked that the Talmudists who spent all their years in Yeshivah X took the position that the woman who scrubbed the floor there before Passover really understood Jewish law better than the sages in Yeshivah Y."

The attitude, deplorable in *yeshivot* but simply indefensible in universities which claim to stand for freedom of inquiry, is commonplace. There is a virtual incapacity of appreciation and informed criticism. Books are rather consigned to oblivion, either by excessive praise or total denigration. Published critical judgment in Jewish learning, all the more so opinions made public through gossip, begin with one or the other of these two propositions, which apply to anyone with whom one does not agree or whom one does not understand: 1. You are insane. 2. You are a charlatan.

How shall we characterize the scholarly results of the present mode of organizing and institutionalizing Jewish learning? One of the most succinct statements of the limitations of the parochial world of Jewish learning points out the following:

> Jewish standards of learning are low, the scholars of standing in the provincial Jewish world are less than nobody elsewhere. The religious seminaries are an unsatisfactory setting because they are sectarian, controlled by unintelligent laity and administrations. Giving money to such institutions for scholarly purposes would only strengthen the clique of monopolistic Jewish scholars, who take in each other's intellectual washing, play the pettiest brand of academic politics, and consider criticism *lèse majesté*. These perpetuate a low standard of learning, since they protect each other's mistakes, use the fear of the "goy" to preserve their academic honor—"criticize us and you'll cause anti-Semitism"—and produce work almost entirely useless for humanistic studies.

Since, on other occasions, I have used nearly the exact words just now quoted. I have to report the date of the document, which is May 23, 1926, and the author, who is Elliot Cohen, writing to Henry Hurwitz (discovered by Harold Wechsler, University of Chicago).

It is not my purpose to deplore what clearly is a pathetic and destructive mode of critical judgment and to point to negligible achievements relative to numbers and pretentions. I rather wish to ask why it is the case that in many, though not all, areas of Jewish learning it is impossible to discover a common ground of discourse, so that the person with whom we disagree is assumed to be either insane or utterly ignorant and incapable of rational thought. Surely practitioners of Jewish learning cannot be thought to be of a different sort of humanity from practitioners of mathematics, classics, anthropology, or history. Whether or not "study of Torah" makes them better people, we cannot take for granted it makes them worse or feeds the natural impulse to treat people in in humane and immoral ways.

I prefer to ask: What has happened to the various university disciplines which evidently has not yet happened to the larger part of the field of Jewish learning? Relying upon the thought of Arnold Thackray and Robert K. Merton ("On Discipline Building: The Paradoxes of George Sarton," *Isis*, 63, pp. 473–95; quoted passages, pp. 474–75), I wish to suggest this: the present state of Jewish learning is the result of the decay of the institutions in which the field once took shape, before the development of new and strong institutions of another kind. My thesis is that the decay of *yeshivot* and other sectarian Jewish seminaries as centers of learning in a primarily intellectual sense—a process not yet described by competent historians, the results of which nonetheless are common knowledge—has not yet been compensated by the development of other cognitive-institutional bases for the work of learning.

Let us begin with the matter of professionalism. Thackray and Merton state:

> In the Western world, universities have most often provided the appropriate context in which a professional identity might be built. Their need of teaching cadres and their tolerance of research have permitted the growth of regular career structures directly or indirectly dependent of the discipline. . . . The existence of career-related opportunities and rewards gives new meaning to an ability to perform well at the intellectual tasks of the discipline. The growth of such socially patterned arrangements inevitably transforms the enterprise on deeper levels. The movement from 'gentlemen' to 'players' is not simply a matter of changes in organization or possible personal reward. It also encompasses a transformation in the images of the discipline and its social and cultural functions. . . .

Thackray and Merton distinguish between the amateur and the professional, the dabbler and the person who devotes his best efforts to his work. What is the trait of a field dominated by amateurs, "gentlemen"? Learning requires time and discipline. The gentleman-scholar, to begin with, is not apt to understand the inner workings of learning, how conclusions are reached—cognitive problems of the nature of evidence, for example. Accordingly, he depends upon opinions, in which he becomes expert, of what this person says about that person, since he is unable to evaluate the work of this person or the opinion of that person. The gentleman-scholar has no serious commitment, moreover, to the subject which he studies. He has some other career, by which he measures his success. Accordingly, to take the self-evident example of the rabbi-scholar, he does not meet the standards of the rabbinate or of scholarship. In each setting he claims to be exempt from professional judgment by virtue of his status in the other. To the rabbis, the rabbi-scholar is a scholar. If he neglects his congregational work, it is because he is judged by some other standard. To the scholars, the rabbi self-evidently is a rabbi, capable of good guesses, perhaps some useful work, but not to be subjected to the rigorous standards of the scholars. When we realize that few Jewish scholars in the nineteenth century were able to make their living through their scholarly work—teaching, writing, research—and that, until the recent past, most books on scholarly subjects in this country were published by men who doubled as pulpit-rabbis simply because scholarly employment was unavailable, we hardly need be surprised at the present state of affairs. In simple terms, Jewish learning in America has been without strong institutional support. Most would-be scholars had no choice but to pursue other careers. Jewish learning was an expression of piety; it might endow the learned man with status of a kind, in some context unrelated to scholarly accomplishment. But it was no way to make a living. That is why scholars and rabbis are interchangeable.

We cannot ignore the fact that some scholars did make a living from their scholarship and enjoyed fair professional opportunities. It was not, however, in universities that they did so, but in Jewish seminaries. The difference between the world of discourse of seminaries and that of universities should not be exaggerated. At the present day, my friends in seminaries insist there is none; I have to believe them. Yet that must be a fairly recent development. For when we examine the life-stories of professional Jewish scholars who taught in seminaries in the first half of the twentieth century, we shall find it difficult to concede that their life-stories run more or less parallel to the life-stories of scholars in universities. The most important American scholar in Jewish learning in the first half of this century is Louis Ginzberg, and his story, happily, is well-documented. It is the story of personal dislocation, of an unresolved conflict of values, much suffering, but great human transcendence, not to mention scholarly achievement. What characterizes Ginzberg, who I believe to be typical, is concern for the opinions of people whom, in fact, he could never satisfy or please. I mean the people he left behind in his movement into Western scholarship. To generalize: one problem of some importance in the formation of Jewish learning in America is the conception that the experience of alienation from a different mode of Jewish learning in Europe must be normative. This produced an exaggerated need both to justify breaking with the past, on the one side, and to meet, even to exceed, the standards of the past, on the other, a conflict in values which severely impeded the development of the scholarly agenda appropriate to the new age and setting of America.

The difficulty in establishing a common framework of discourse, shared criteria for what is good and what is bad, even widely-accepted agenda of what work is worth doing—that difficulty is evidence of the primitive state of the institutionalization of Jewish learning. The *bittul* to which Rabbi Fasman refers testifies to the effects of an institutional flaw. Following Thackeray and Merton, I may call that flaw the absence of a cognitive identity. These authors refer to "the set of shifts that a field of learning experiences as it changes from being a diffuse, unfocused area of inquiry, at best tangential to the true intellectual concerns of its occasional votaries, to being a conceptually discrete discipline, able to command its own tools, techniques, methodologies, intellectual orientations, and problematics. This creation of a cognitive identity is only one facet of the institutionalization of a field of learning." To repeat what I said earlier, the reason that we are unable to talk with one another is not our ill-will or stupidity. We have failed, to date, to transform Jewish learning from its present diffuse, unfocused, and undisciplinary character to a conceptually discrete discipline (or set of disciplines), with its own tools, techniques, methodologies, intellectual orientations, and problematics.

It is this structural flaw, and not the personality-quirk of this person or the "ignorance" of that person, which lies at the foundations of our problem. For, having left *yeshivot*, Jewish learning did not have the opportunity to make its way into universities. For a long time it has persisted in the limbo of seminaries pretending to be *yeshivot*, on the one side, or pretending to have no deep commitment to the wide range of Jewish learning, on the other. In the former category obviously is the Jewish Theological Seminary of America under earlier management, and in the latter is the long generation of Hebrew Union College marked by predominant interest in Assyriology and other aspects of Semitics, clinical and social psychology, and other disciplines tangential to the inherited disciplines of Jewish learning, and a certain disinterest in the agendum of the recent past in *yeshivot*. I stress that both great centers of learning have entered a new stage in their history, and those of us in universities can only benefit from the practical power represented by appointments and public recognition, exercised in a constructive way, by those faculties. Their problems and our problems as educators are not the same; but as scholars we face an identical task.

II

Let me now spell out the structural fault to which I have alluded, namely, the failure of Jewish learning in America to formulate a cognitive identify (in the language of Thackray and Merton), or a commonly accepted set of modes of thought and inquiry. First, let us briefly consider the modes of thought characteristic of the *yeshivot*-world, then ask about those ways of analyzing problems commonplace in contemporary university-scholarship (including, I repeat, scholarship carried on in the university-mode of thought, but in seminaries). Our question is whether the inherited patterns of thinking are appropriate, i.e., functional, to our present setting; and if, as I shall argue, they are only marginally relevant, can we specify the sort of thinking which is both functional and relevant?

How did scholars in *yeshivot* formulate their work—the problems they chose to solve, the way in which they distinguished important from unimportant matters, good from bad solutions, and the like?

In a word, the mode of thought characteristic of the classical commentators to the sacred literature of rabbinic Judaism is ahistorical, exegetical, deductive, if not theological, at least rigidly canonical, and discrete. It is not historical, comprehensive, inductive, broad in focus and unlimited by canon, or concerned with larger structures and even generalizations of social weight and relevance. What people did and still do in *yeshivot* is study Talmud, codes, and commentaries to the Talmud, in ascending order of importance. Their mode of study is to proceed line by line, verse by verse. Their task is to assimilate what the text says and, more important, rapidly to enter into its complexities, as laid forth in primarily logical terms by the commentaries (which accounts for the stress on commentaries). The supposition of all learning is that we deal with a unitary text. Everything is to be shown to be harmonious with everything else; every principle, every authority, is to be demonstrated to harmonize with every other principle and authority. The texts and the laws they contain are to be shown as testifying to the presence of a prior, even primordial unity of conception.

Texts are not to be analyzed in the supposition that they have a history, that they did not always say what they now are presumed to be telling us. Authorities—as everyone knows—existed under the aspect of eternity, so that Aqiva may not be allowed to disagree with Ashi or Abbaye, and the second-century Judah must be shown to conform to the opinions of the third-century one. The social, economic, and cultural setting of the various authorities, of course, is not allowed to enter the exegetical process. As for that process, it involves the interpretation of the smallest possible units of thought, with slight regard to specific context, but with much attention to general relationships to other small units of thought. The closest attention is paid to the meanings of words and phrases, but the construction of a larger picture—the positing of four or five thoughts, arranged consecutively and in logical sequence, the search for generalization and meaning—that process tends to be grossly neglected. Finally, "new" ideas are posited in advance, then deductively "proved." Inductive inquiry and speculation are virtually absent.

This cognitive system, highly functional to its setting and social tasks in traditional Jewish culture, is carried over in the main achievements of Jewish learning in seminaries over the past fifty or seventy years. Using Louis Ginzberg as our example, we may point that he did new things in old ways—a commentary to the Yerushalmi, a text not much studied in *yeshivot*, but a commentary constructed in both the forms and the intellectual conventions familiar in *yeshivot*; historical essays which posit a theory, reasonable enough to be sure, and then illustrate the theory endlessly, a kind of high level begging of the question.

We need not overstate the usefulness of these modes of thought to the cultural setting which produced them. But it is time to observe that they are not the modes of thought common in universities. University studies in the humanities, while based upon sound exegesis of texts and careful philology, are not limited to the inherited canons of a particular religious tradition. Equally obvious: university scholarship in the humanities is keenly aware of historical considerations in the exegesis of texts. Still more obvious: university studies tend to be inductive, not deductive. The effort is to construct a large picture, not merely to make discrete points following an agendum laid out by some ancient redactor, an agendum consisting of a text to be studied, line by line and page by page. A course in Talmud normally consists of reading one page after another, with appropriate commentary. A course in Martin Luther, by contrast will involve reading more than one page after another of Luther's writings. The larger heuristic and hermeneutical questions are never raised in *yeshivot*. University scholars make the effort to uncover how things work, to get inside, or behind, the opaque surfaces of texts. Accordingly, they do not begin with the assumption of the text's veracity, whether historical or philosophical, but with a set of critical questions.

It follows that generalization is important. Coherent and cogent ideas are welcome. Four or five consecutive thoughts, logically arranged, are demanded, and, while requisite attention is paid to detail, it is also understood that a proposition must be examined whole. Details are nuanced, some important, some less so, in the analysis and criticism of that whole proposition. These are some of the ways in which classical Jewish modes of thought and contemporary university modes of thought differ from one another. And I have not even alluded to the other world of thought—the one supplied by the social sciences—utterly beyond the knowledge and appreciation of traditional Jewish circles, and yet so interesting to university scholars, including those in the humanities.

Let me summarize, I propose as a fair criterion for the vitality of a field of learning the possibility of reasoned discourse, in accord with an established methodology, about a common set of questions. Many fields exhibit the capacity for fruitful and fructifying discourse. Jewish learning in both *yeshivot* and universities is characterized by a different sort of discourse, which, in accord with the examples I have adduced, would seem to be irresponsible, trivial, and expressive of deep disdain. Books are not read before they are criticized, then proscribed. *Yeshivah* scholars and university scholars alike seem to find it difficult to talk with one another. Why should this be the case? On the assumption that scholars in the field of Jewish learning are neither more nor less moral or stupid than scholars in other fields, I suggest that the cause is structural. The institutions to which the classical modes of Jewish thought were functional and appropriate have decayed. The new settings for Jewish learning have yet to be characterized by modes of thought and discourse functional to those new settings.

Yeshivot and Jewish seminaries treat freedom of thought as heresy. Intellectual conformity is interpreted as intelligence. The life of the intellect has been turned into a series of rituals, lifeless and without substance. Critical judgment consists in sharing gossip about which authority deprecated which other authority. Students are kept in a state of dependence upon their teachers, not taught to do, on their own, what their teachers do. That political conception of learning is characteristic of the pulpit-rabbis, who, not knowing the issues of learning, want only to know the personalities, the gossip. But it tends not to be wholly absent even among the scholars themselves. Jewish learning, in the exact sense of Thackray and Merton, is diffuse, unfocused, unspecialized, conceptually without definition, without tools, techniques, methodologies, intellectual orientations, problematics: it lacks a cognitive identity.

This proposition, I argue, is shown in the persistence of modes of thinking which have outlived their relevance to the contemporary intellectual life as it is lived in universities (and in Jewish seminaries, it is claimed, as well). No other intellectual methodologies have replaced the *yeshivah* or seminary ones, except for isolated individuals, who, in consequence, find themselves in an uncomfortable situation. I need not dwell on that point. But it is a measure of the intellectual weakness of the field of Jewish learning in America that people find it possible to talk with one another about scholarly matters only with great difficulty. In the main the common preference is to condemn what one does not understand, even more to vilify the person who says something one does not understand or accept. I can think of no more telling criterion for the strength or weakness of the field than the mode of criticism of another person's ideas: criticism of the main point and its foundations, or criticism of trivialities. Journals in Jewish learning which print book-reviews consisting of lists of "mistakes" and misprints, but containing not even fifty words on the theory of a book, are common.

III

Thus far I have tried only to describe the present situation. I have stressed that we confront a considerable cognitive flaw, a major transition in the institutionalization of Jewish learning. Let me now briefly allude to factors which are irrelevent to the processes of scholarship but which exert strong influence on Jewish learning in particular.

One powerful influence on Jewish learning is the conviction that the act of learning bears more than intellectual consequences. It represents a religious or personal affirmation, both in itself and in its cognitive results. Accordingly, the results of scholarship are measured against non-scholarly criteria. If we come up with a picture found distasteful for theological or polemical reasons, we have to explain away the picture we have found. A powerful apologetic motif characterizes much of Jewish learning and constitutes a massive obstacle in the face of scholarly progress. "Loyalty to the Jewish people"—that is, apologetics—conflicts with devotion to objective search for facts, for truth.

A second, and corollary, factor is the personal engagement of scholars in their work, in a way more or less without parallel in other areas. Historians or mathematicians are deeply interested in their work. But historians or mathematicians rarely hope to work out their personal and existential situation through their scholarly activities in the ways in which, through scholarship, Jewish scholars of Jewish studies work out personal issues extraneous to learning. For Jewish scholarship is not merely a subject, but a mode of expression of one's Jewishness, for nearly everyone in the field who to begin with is Jewish. And, it follows, the necessity to integrate the area of Jewish learning into other areas of learning through common disciplinary approaches is perceived as a kind of assimilation, a shedding of whatever shreds of Jewish identity may yet remain. The so-called "vertical" approach, which treats Jewish studies as a continuum from the very beginnings to the present day, not only rationalizes a fair measure of incompetence and superficiality. It also guarantees that people will form opinions on a wide range of topics which they have not critically investigated so that they will, perforce, ignore the cultural issues facing the Jews at any given period or place. This canonical conception of the field is the counterpart, in scholarship, of the stress upon Jewish particularity and isolation in political, cultural, and social life. It is self-evidently contrary to the primary convictions of the humanities in particular, and the world of universities in general.

I am not inclined to think the situation will change in the near future. The reason is that the university as the institutional setting for the field of Jewish learning is new. People will have to spend careers in universities, set examples for future teachers. Jewish scholars will need time to adjust to the climate of tolerance and freedom, not to mention courtesy and collegiality, characteristic of universities and not characteristic of the field of Jewish studies as now practiced in both *yeshivot* and universities. When freedom of thought and of inquiry has become the norm, when Jewish scholars have discovered that there is much to be learned from other people, both in their field and in other fields, when the intolerance, petty-mindedness, and nit-picking of the Jewish scholars give way to genuine intellectual curiosity and intellectual inquiry, then the cognitive identify of which I have spoken will begin to take shape. That will take a very long time. I do not expect that our generation will live to contribute to the interesting work to be undertaken when Jewish learning now located *in* universities, becomes truly part and parcel *of* universities.

7. THE MISHNAH AND THE SMUDGEPOTS
Or Why, Where There's Smoke, There Isn't Always Fire

The heated debates surrounding the character and meaning of the Mishnah, ca. 200 C.E., the first document of Judaism after the Hebrew Scripture, present a puzzle. Why, one wonders, should people get so excited about a law-code seventeen hundred years old, laws most of which no one observes in their original form? Yet in the recent past, two librarians, on either side of the Atlantic, heap fire and brimstone on the head of someone whose views on the Mishnah they reject.[1] Rhetoric out of all proportion to the scholarly, even arcane, character of the issues draws attention to the victim's motivations, his sinister, dishonorable purposes. In the name of making academic points, the critics settle theological scores. The smoke of ad hominem attacks on competence and the stench of cheap shots[2] obscure such flame of truth as may yet burn. And, in point of fact, some may wish to conclude that, as in Joe McCarthy's time, where there's smoke, there's a smudgepot.

If we wish to interpret the debate and its issues, we do well, first of all, to ask whether it is only in our day that the Mishnah has defined the focus for such rancor, so acrimonious a version of scholarly discussion. We seek perspective on the remarkably heated character of discourse, on the sounds and fury of a war about what are, in point of fact, trivialities, facts of a long gone age and their interpretation. Christian on-lookers to the brawl propose that, anyhow, that's how Jews argue, another example of that "Jewish excess of emotions" that our gentile neighbors deplore. But if we concede that Jewish scholars treat scholarly issues as a blood sport, we still must wonder why in other areas of Jewish learning, cool, near-gentile restraint prevails. We should look in vain for personal imprecations to fill up articles on such topics as the definition of midrash, the interpretation of Maimonides' doctrine of the Messiah, or even the history of Qabbalah in Spain. And if people propose that, because the Mishnah constitutes the first document of the Oral Torah, debates about the history and character of the Mishnah gain their intensity and their sour spirit from the presence of theological poison, two facts intervene. First, an equivalent spirit does not

[1] Cf. Hyam Maccoby, "Jacob Neusner's Mishnah," *Midstream* 1984, 30:24–32.

[2] Shaye J. D. Cohen, "Jacob Neusner, Mishnah, and Counter-Rabbinics," *Conservative Judaism* 1983, 37:48–63.

characterize Jewish discourse on biblical problems. Second, parties to the present debate to begin with are not Orthodox but Reform and Conservative, so on the face of it no fiercely-defended doctrinal issue can account for the fury of the fray.

Then let the truth be told. Perhaps it is really the personality of one or another, or all, of the participants to the dispute that accounts for acrimony about neutral matters of fact or even mere interpretation. So a plague on all our heads? That argument, of course, can never find decisive refutation. But it loses all credibility when we revert, as I said, to how, in past times, people carried on their discussions about the Mishnah in particular. For, in point of fact, at the very beginnings of modern Jewish scholarship, a century and a quarter ago, people conducted their disputes about the history and character of the Mishnah exactly as they do today. And, I would argue, no interpretation of the way people debate the issues at hand today can fail to draw the parallel and ask for an explanation of that parallel.

I

I refer, in particular, to one of the founding documents of modern Jewish scholarship, Zechariah Frankel's *Darkhé Hammishnah* (*The Ways of the Mishnah*), originally published in Leipzig in German in 1859, and republished as recently as 1959 in Tel Aviv in Hebrew. Frankel, who was born in 1801 in Prague and died in Breslau in 1875, served as a rabbi, mainly in Dresden, then in Breslau as founding director of the Jewish Theological Seminary. He enjoys credit as the founder of what is called "positive-historical Judaism," to which present day Conservative Judaism traces its lineage. What this meant in practice, in synagogue life, was introducing a choir, organ, and German-language sermons. But he rejected the Reform rabbis' changes, which he held arbitrary. His earlier scholarly work, proving that a Jew's oath can be trusted (1846) and demonstrating the antiquity of Jewish Law, somewhat later, excited no great animosity. *Darkhé Hammishnah* did.

Nothing in the outline of the work on the surface explains why anyone should get excited about the book. Frankel proposed to define the Mishnah and explain the nature of its contents, treat the halakhah in relationship to the Torah, and explain why halakhah changes. He reviewed the lives of authorities of the Mishnah in a long sequence of thumb-nail sketches, made up of compilations of tales about the several principal figures. This biographical (in context: historical) exercise covers a third of whole. Then Frankel treats the history of the formation of the Mishnah, its text, literary character, and structure. His special interest, in all this, was to prove the antiquity of the Oral Torah. This he does by demonstrating that, in content, the Oral Torah—that is, the Mishnah—dates back to a very early period. In the words of Joel Gereboff, "By citing examples . . . , Frankel asserts that the development of the Mishnah was a conservative process. Nothing from the past was changed . . . later generations worked systematically to build on what they had received."[3] So much for the character of the book and its argument: deeply conservative, if anything an attack on Reform Judaism, entirely consistent with the author's earlier interests and publications.

The response to the book was enormous. Samson Raphael Hirsch, for the Orthodox opposition, and Shelomo Rappoport, for the defense, engaged in vigorous and heated debate. About what? Hirsch focused on the critical issue: Was the Mishnah the work of man or God? Again Gereboff: "The discussion centered about three points: the origin of the halakhah, divine or in the Great Assembly? The origin of the hermeneutical principles—divine or human? The meaning of 'a law revealed to Moses from Sinai,' a divine or very old or self-evident law?" What had gone wrong was simple. Frankel had treated the Mishnah as the work of men. He even interpreted matters in a way other than is found in the Babylonian Talmud, turning, instead, to the Palestinian one.

In fact Frankel presented too small a target. The Seminary he headed bore the brunt of attacks. One of his critics stands for them all: "There has arisen in the land a new group of people who do not trust in the truth of faith, but have followed the desires of their hearts. They have vented their disgusting spirit upon the Torah, which they have not accepted as Mosaic and now will do the same to the Talmud," so Shelomo Klein. When this kind of splenetic outburst takes the place of serious criticism, it is for one reason only. The critic, terribly angry to begin with, cannot either join the issue as framed by the author or find some other. But the critic here was right—not about Frankel's "disgusting spirit," but about the issue at hand. Frankel really had done what the critics said. He had treated the Mishnah as the work of men. Why the violence?

What happened between the time of Frankel's earlier work, beginning in the 1840's, and the publication of his book on the Mishnah? The question seems pertinent, for the violent reception of the ideas in the later book presents a puzzle in light of the irenic response to the essentially congruent premises revealed in the earlier work. In the words of Bernhard Brilling, "The first modern Jewish theological seminary, the Juedisch-Theologisches Seminar, was established in Breslau by Zechariah Frankel in 1854. With its celebrated library it became a center of Jewish scholarship. . . . It also published the first comprehensive Jewish learned journal, *Monatschrift für Geschichte and Wissenschaft des Judentums*."[4] So what Frankel had done in the years just before publishing his great work was to establish

---

[3] Joel Gereboff, "The Pioneer: Zecharias Frankel," in J. Neusner, ed., *The Modern Study of the Mishnah* (Leiden, 1974), pp. 59–75.

[4] See his article, "Breslau," *Encyclopaedia Judaica* 4:1355.

two things, first, a new kind of institution for Judaic learning, and second, a new type of medium for public discourse in Judaic learning. In these two ways, Frankel had defined a new social setting for Judaic studies, different from the established one in important and obvious ways.

The new school was not individual but on-going; it conducted an organized curriculum; it pursued subjects (whether of Jewish interest or not) earlier ignored; it represented a viewpoint deriving from a source other than the established yeshiva-world-view of the same time and region. The new journal, in German, accorded with the standards of public discourse not of that same yeshiva-world but of the university-world of Germany. It was meant, for one thing to be judicious, civil, and restrained, virtues lacking in the home-circumstance of the yeshiva-world. Frankel's reply to his critics is a case in point: "People should read the book [*The Ways of the Mishnah*] without presuppositions. It is a book on the development of the halakhah and the Mishnah and not on theology. Attacks should be made against the book and not against its author or his Seminary." But that, of course, was the point.

II

If we may generalize from a single case, what I think we see is a shift in the social and institutional foundations of a field of study as much as a change in the modes of thought or the paradigms of learning. It was one thing for Frankel to cite the Talmud of the Land of Israel (the "Palestinian Talmud") instead of the Babylonian one. People could even swallow his interest in the Septuagint, the Greek translation of Scripture, and other studies outside of the range of the rabbinic writings of antiquity. But when he asked a set of questions formerly not raised, about the historical, and therefore human, origins of the Mishnah, and when he raised those questions in the sanctuary of an institution beyond the power of the yeshiva-world and in the context of a journal not controlled by that world's values, that was another matter. In publishing his book on the Mishnah, as I said the critical document of the faith, the first constituent of that Oral Torah that defined Judaism, Frankel threw down the gauntlet.

The heat of debate, the uninhibited personal attacks—these expressed not power but pathetic weakness. The other side could not argue with Frankel, nor, still worse, could the critics get to him. He could not be dismissed or ignored or merely boycotted or humiliated. These modes of public pressure lacking, the enemy on the right, the Orthodox, had to resort to saying what they really thought. It did no good. Frankel's work defined the program of scholarship for the next century. His critics could do nothing about it, because they could not persuade the people who received Frankel's work—his colleagues, his students, and those that carried on from them. The enemies crept back into the protected domain of their own institutions, their own social setting, their own media of public discourse. They had no choice. Scholarship continued on its way without them. Today there are Orthodox who defend Frankel as Orthodox.

III

This long detour through events of a century and a quarter ago places into perspective accusations that someone holds the views he does, and expresses them, so that he can get a job in a university (and an obscure, unimportant one at that)! Why make one's place of employment an issue, let alone a mode of explaining scholarly views one is constrained, after all, to refute? And what sort of scholarly refutation takes the form of pointing to the source of an opponent's paycheck? In other words, you have to wonder why someone would bother to construct such a puzzling argument (among many curiosities).

In this context, I am reminded of yet another mode of refutation, equally feeble, which consists of listing misprints in a book, on the one side, or catalogues of trivial errors, on the other—always joined by cries of "worthless" and "comic."[5] After all, errors are there to be corrected, but the work goes on. It is not as if, by reason of a misprint or a trivial error, one that scarcely affects the meaning of a paragraph, let alone a page, someone went out and committed murder or adultery or even ate pork! At issue in scholarship is only learning, that is, a labor of trying to grasp and make sense of the text and of the world.

Yet that, of course, vastly misrepresents matters. At issue in scholarship, when it comes to Judaism, are many things, and least among them, it often seems, is the pursuit of natural curiosity about why things were, or are, the way they seem rather than some other way. It is for good reason that the Mishnah forms the centerpiece of debate again and again. Why so? Because it indeed is the first document of Judaism beyond the Hebrew Scriptures. Everything we know about the world from the end of the Hebrew Bible to the formation of the first writings

---

[5] See Saul Lieberman, "A Tragedy or a Comedy?" *Journal of the American Oriental Society* 1984, 104:315–19. In this context, I take note that Lieberman's posthumous review was circulated prior to publication, by the book editor of the JAOS, for about a year. Hearing about it, on April 19, 1983, I wrote to him, "It seems to me out of the question to reply at all to a dead man; I cannot imagine how it could be done with dignity and decency. If you choose to print the review and if you wish a comment from me, it is as follows: 'People do not reply to a lion after [his] death,' Y. Git. 9:1." Lieberman's corrections are valuable and appreciated, in line with Proverbs 9:8–9. I list them in an appendix to my *Talmud* Vol. 23, the first available volume. The rest is covered by my statement of April 19, 1983.

of Judaism, beginning in ca. 200 C.E., derives, to begin with, from the Mishnah and from the writings that flow from the Mishnah.

So when paradigms shift, as they have, and the social foundations of learning change, as they have, we return to the original arena of Judaic discourse, the Mishnah. Scholarly debates today take the place of theological ones in medieval times; at issue in a misprint or a mistranslation is not correcting secular error but demonstrating sin and heresy.

IV

Then why the furor just now, just here? Since Frankel's work came under attack only as part of a full scale assault against his seminary, we have to ask what institutional difference defines today's disputes and accounts for the heat and rancor. Phrased in this way, the question answers itself. Just as Frankel's approach to learning, his interest in questions of history, accorded with the character and requirements of the new institution he had founded, so the new approaches to the problem of the Mishnah come to full expression in a new setting for Judaic studies, secular universities.

It is no accident, in my view, that when people ask new questions, they do so in a new setting, for new types of students, and in a new medium of discourse. People in the Conservative and Reform Judaic seminaries take deep offense not only at what is said, but, as their rhetoric tells us, also at who says it, to whom, and where he prints it.

It is in a university. It is to a neutral audience, made up not only of insiders, such as rabbis. It is in a book published not by a rabbinical press or a Jewish publisher but by a university press of premier standing. And, the important point for last: the issues also are new ones. And they derive from the secular humanities of today's university discourse. Let me explain.

In *Judaism: The Evidence of the Mishnah*, I analyze a single document, essentially out of all relationship to the other documents of the larger canon of authoritative and holy books of Judaism. I read that document on its own. This is just as scholars of the history of the American Constitution read the Constitution not only in light of all of the court decisions of the past two hundred years but also in its own setting and context. Why does that decision, to read a book all by itself (with the clear plan of reading other books of the same canon one by one) make so much trouble?

When we take up a single document in the canon of Judaism and propose to describe, analyze, and interpret that text in particular, we violate the lines of order and system that have characterized earlier studies of these same documents. Until now, people have tended to treat all of the canonical texts as testimonies to a single system and structure, that is, to "Judaism." What sort of testimonies texts provide varies according to the interest of the scholars, students, and saints who study them. Scholars look for meanings of words and phrases, better versions of a text. For them all canonical documents equally serve as a treasury of philological facts and variant readings. Students also look for the sense of words and phrases and follow a given phrase hither and yon, as their teachers direct them on their treasure hunt. Saints study all texts equally, looking for God's will and finding testimonies to God in each component of the Torah of Moses our Rabbi.

Among none of these circles, Orthodox, Reform, Conservative, Israeli alike, will the discrete description, analysis, and interpretation of a single text make sense. Why not? Because all texts ordinarily are taken to form a common statement, "Torah" in the mythic setting, "Judaism" in the theological one. From the accepted perspective the entire canon of Judaism—"the one whole Torah of Moses, our rabbi"—equally and at every point testifies to the entirety of Judaism. Why so? Because all documents in the end form components of a single system. Each makes its contribution to the whole. If, therefore, we wish to know what "Judaism" or, more accurately, "the Torah," teaches on any subject, we are able to draw freely on sayings relevant to that subject wherever they occur in the entire canon of Judaism. Guided only by the taste and judgment of the great sages of the Torah, as they have addressed the question at hand, we thereby describe "Judaism."

Accordingly, as Judaism comes to informed expression in the Judaic pulpit, in the Judaic classroom, above all in the lives and hearts and minds of Jews loyal to Judaism, all parts of the canon of Judaism speak equally authoritatively. All parts, all together, present us with one harmonious world-view and homogeneous way of life, one Torah ("Judaism") for all Israel. That view of "the Torah," that is to say, of the canon of Judaism, characterizes every organized movement within Judaism as we now know it, whether Reform or Orthodox, whether Reconstructionist or Conservative, whether in the Exile (diaspora) or in the State of Israel. How so? Among circles of Judaism indifferent to considerations of time and place, anachronism and context, every document, whenever brought to closure, testifies equally to that single system. For those circles Judaism emerges at a single moment ("Sinai"), but comes to expression in diverse times and places, so that any composition that falls into the category of Torah serves, without further differentiation, to tell us about the substance of Judaism, its theology and law.

V

For a person such as my self, by contrast, engaged in such an inquiry into the historical formation of Judaism studied through the analysis of the unfolding literary evidence of the canon, documents stand in three relationships to one another and to the system of which they form part, that is, to "Judaism," as a whole. They are relationships of autonomy, connection, and continuity.

Each document is to be seen all by itself, that is, as *autonomous* of all others.

Each document, again as a matter of theory, is to be examined for its relationships, as *connected*, with other documents universally regarded as falling into the same classification, as Torah.

And, finally, each document is to be allowed to take its place as part of the undifferentiated aggregate of documents that, all together, constitute the canon of Judaism, that is to say, "Torah." It is shown to form part of a *continuity*.

Simple logic makes self-evident the proposition that, if a document comes down to us within its own framework, as a complete book with a beginning, middle, and end, in preserving that book, the canon presents us with a document on its own and not solely as part of a larger composition or construct. So we too see the document as it reaches us, that is, as autonomous.

If, second, a document contains materials shared verbatim or in substantial content with other documents of its classification, or if one document refers to the contents of other documents, then the several documents that clearly wish to engage in conversation with one another have to address one another. That is to say, we have to seek for the marks of connectedness, asking for the meaning of these connections.

Finally, since, as I said at the outset, the community of the faithful of Judaism, in all of the contemporary expressions of Judaism, concur that documents held to be authoritative constitute one whole, seamless "Torah," that is, a complete and exhaustive statement of God's will for Israel and humanity, we take as our further task the description of the whole out of the undifferentiated testimony of all of its parts. These components in the theological context are viewed, as is clear, as equally authoritative for the composition of the whole: one, continuous system. In taking up such a question, we address a problem not of theology alone, though it is a correct theological conviction, but one of description, analysis, and interpretation of an entirely historical order.

In my view the various documents of the canon of Judaism produced in late antiquity demand a hermeneutic altogether different from the one of homogenization and harmonization, the ahistorical and anti-contextual one I have rejected. It is one that does not harmonize but that differentiates. It is a hermeneutic shaped to teach us how to read the texts at hand one by one and in a particular context, exactly in the way in which we read any other text bearing cultural and social insight. The texts stand not as self-evidently important but only as examples, sources of insight for a quite neutral inquiry. Let me spell out what I think is at issue between the established hermeneutic and the one I propose. Why in universities and not in seminaries do I find my audience?

VI

The three key-words of the inherited hermeneutic are *continuity*, *uniqueness*, and *survival*. Scholars who view the texts as continuous with one another seek what is unique in the system formed by the texts as a whole. With the answer to what is unique, they propose to explain the survival of Israel, the Jewish people. Hence: continuity, uniqueness, survival.

The words to encapsulate the hermeneutic I espouse are these: *description, analysis*, and *interpretation*. I am trying to learn how to *describe* the constituents of the canon, viewed individually, each in its distinctive context. I wish to discover appropriate *analytical* tools, questions to lead me from description of one text to comparison and contrast between two or more texts of the canon. Only at the end do I address the question of *interpretation*: how do all of the texts of the canon at hand flow together into a single continuous statement, a "Judaism."

Within the inherited hermeneutic of continuity, survival, and uniqueness, the existence of the group defines the principal concern, an inner-facing one, hence the emphasis on uniqueness in quest, in continuities, for the explanation of survival. Within the proposed hermeneutic of description, analysis, and interpretation, by contrast, the continued survival of a "unique" group does not frame the issue. For my purposes, it is taken for granted, for the group is not the main thing at all. That is an insider's question. The problematic emerges from without. What I want to know is not how and why the group survived so as to help it survive some more. It is how to describe the society and culture contained within, taken as a given, how to interpret an enduring world-view and way of life, expressed by the artifacts in hand. How did, and does, the group work? That is an issue of benign curiosity.

So I claim that the results of the literary inquiry will prove illuminating for the study of society and culture. I have now to explain why I think so. The answer lies in our will and capacity to generalize, out of details, a judgment on a broad issue of culture, as it is exemplified in the small problem at hand. The issue here is secular.

True, I too ask how the components of the canon as a whole form a continuity. I wonder why this document in particular survived to speak for the whole. But for me the answers to these questions generate theories, promise insight for the study of other canonical religions. So far as I shall succeed, it will be because I can learn from these other canonical religions. I have tried to learn from, and also to teach something to, those who study the history, the thought, the social reality, of religions that, like Judaism, form enduring monuments to the power of humanity to endure and to prevail so far. Judaism presents a mere example of a truth beyond itself, a truth of humanistic interest.

VII

Let us, finally, turn to the substance of the debate and see whether we can sort out what matters from what is merely personal or mostly incoherent (as, alas, happens to be the case). What bothers the critics most of all? It is the very definition of the work, and, to the critics' credit, they do pick out the main innovation. What I have done is to ask a very simple question. If we read the Mishnah all by itself, without reference to any other corpus of writing, what sort of system, if any, so we find in the document?

To show, first of all, that that is the critical issue, I point to the substantive and entirely relevant argument. One critic takes the view that one cannot look at a single document in isolation. Why not? All of the rabbinic literature constitutes a single mass, each element present among all others (thus: continuity). Another critic takes umbrage (shades of Klein and Hirsch) that someone has read the Mishnah out of phase with the Babylonian Talmud (as though Maimonides did not do the same thing in his Mishnah-commentary nearly eight hundred years ago!). Why is that wrong? Because, again, we should not read the Mishnah by itself but only as it has been read through the eyes of the authors of documents that received the Mishnah, and particularly, the Babylonian Talmud, completed four hundred years after the closure of the Mishnah.

And, finally, we are told that since the documents of the rabbinic cannon intersect and overlap, as they do, we must "always" read them "synoptically," meaning in light of one another. If these criticisms prove valid, then the very notion of asking about the system, the "Judaism," of the Mishnah in particular rests upon a totally wrong premise. One need not read a book about "Judaism: the evidence of the Mishnah," because the Mishnah by itself cannot testify to any system, any "Judaism," by itself.

When we turn to the Mishnah itself, the document does exhibit traits we associate with autonomous documents. That is to say, if you study the Mishnah from outside to inside, seeing it whole and not merely as a scrapbook or collection of bits and pieces, the document turns out to follow a cogent program and to make a coherent set of statements. We know that fact on the basis of two traits of the Mishnah, its formal character, its substantial message.

The language of the Mishnah follows patterns. These patterns repeat themselves, often in groups of three or five examples of a single pattern.

The substance of a set of three or five such examples is cogent. How so? Each of the five makes the same point that the others do. If you take up a sizable piece of the document, then, and trace the units of thought— that is, the groups of examples of the same point—you discover an interesting thing. Sets of three or five examples of one basic notion resort to a single distinctive pattern of language. Then, when a new point is made by a new set of examples, it will come to expression in a pattern different from the one before. This is a round-about way of explaining that, in the Mishnah, when the subject changes, so does the rhetorical pattern.

Now that trait of speech, the matching of rhetoric and topic, is so pervasive in the Mishnah that we must wonder whether the document stands by itself, or whether the Mishnah is simply another instance in which rabbis, wherever and whenever they lived, expressed their ideas. If that striking trait proves commonplace in many writings, then, on merely formal grounds, we cannot treat the Mishnah as special and ask about its ideas, its system in particular. In point of fact, however, only the Mishnah is so formulated. Its closest companion, the Tosefta, a collection of supplementary teachings concerning the topics and rules found in the Mishnah, is not. And no other rabbinic writing, from the Mishnah through the Bavli four centuries later, exhibits those distinctive traits of formalization that the Mishnah does. (Many documents produce other traits of careful formulation, but not the Mishnah's.)

One may well argue that the mere fact that a document is written in a special way does not prove the writing is special. That is indeed so. A second, well-known fact does make us suppose that the Mishnah follows its own program not only in form but also in meaning. It is the simple datum that, after the Mishnah, no other sustained piece of writing takes up exactly the program of topics that the Mishnah's authors treat. The Mishnah is composed of six divisions, on six principal topics: agriculture, the calendar, women and the family, civil law, the cult, and purity. The heirs of the Mishnah in the Talmud of the Land of Israel (ca. 400 C.E.) ignored the fifth and sixth divisions. The heirs of the Mishnah in the Talmud of Babylonia (ca. 600 C.E.) skipped the first and the sixth. Only two important heirs to the Mishnah follow the Mishnah's program, the authors of the Tosefta, and Maimonides a thousand years later.

VIII

These rather obvious and simple considerations justify asking what the Mishnah, when read whole and complete, appears to say as a cogent message.

But what of the repeated criticism, that it is improper to read the Mishnah by itself simply because the Mishnah forms part of a larger whole? A classic statement of this view, not with reference to the Mishnah in particular, comes from Lawrence H. Schiffman: "This system, composed of interlocking and re-interlocking parts possessed of an organic connection one to another, is never really divisible."[6] If that were so, then I have sinned grievously in taking up not only one of the parts, but the principal one, distinguishing it from all others, and reading it on its own.

But do all the parts turn out to be indivisible and indistinguishable from one another? That remains to be demonstrated. The critics assuredly stand on firm ground—so a superficial glance would suggest—in seeing as intersecting the rabbinic documents of late antiquity. From the Mishnah, to the Tosefta, the Talmud of the Land of Israel, the Talmud of Babylonia, the Mekhilta, Sifra, two Sifres, Genesis Rabbah, Leviticus Rabbah, Pesiqta de R. Kahana, and on and on, sayings and stories do circulate hither and yon. The meaning of the fact that a saying may make its way from one document to the next awaits systematic investigation.

We have, for example, to ask how much of a document must be shared with some other(s) before that document loses all integrity and melts into an undifferentiated mass? If the bulk of a document is shared with others, then we may see the book at hand as a mere container, lacking all power to shape the traits or change the taste of what is poured into it. A text is then merely a context, a place for storing things, so to speak.

We must also demonstrate, to the contrary, that when a document makes use of a saying or a story, it is for a purpose, part of a larger program, distinctive to the document at hand. In that case, a text possesses integrity and enjoys autonomy, even though, at some points, it is concentric with some other text(s).

IX

Obviously, the issues before us demand detailed sifting and sorting out. Generalizations prove premature, when each of the texts has not been analyzed in detail, both by itself and in relationship to others. I have conducted such analysis of integrity in a systematic way on three texts, the Mishnah, the Tosefta, and Leviticus Rabbah. Each exhibits its own quite distinctive traits. The Mishnah's authors cite nothing but Scripture, and then only occasionally. The Tosefta's authors depend heavily upon the Mishnah, which they cite verbatim and upon which they depend for the order and organization of their ideas. Leviticus Rabbah only rarely goes over materials found in any text prior to its own day (though the later composition, Pesiqta de R. Kahana, borrows heavily from Leviticus Rabbah). On that basis, we surely cannot generalize

[6] Lawrence H. Schiffman, *Sectarian Law in the Dead Sea Scrolls. Courts, Testimony, and the Penal Code* (Chico, 1983), p. 3.

that "every" document must "always" be read in the light of every other document.

When, at the end, critics ask why I do not read the Mishnah in light of everything said by everybody from the publication of the Mishnah to the day before yesterday, my answer is simple. Why should I? Does anybody in philosophy read Plato only through the eyes of the neo-Platonists? And who, any more, insists that the Hebrew Bible be read as Rashi dictates we should read it—except to understand Rashi? The history of the exegetical tradition of the Mishnah yields the intellectual history of the legal tradition of Judaism from the time of the Mishnah onward, an extraordinarily interesting story.

I know, because in my commentary,[7] I followed the whole of the exegetical tradition of the Mishnah and of the Tosefta for the Division of Purities and published twenty-two volumes on that division, dealing with the important received exegeses of each passage in sequence. I should be the last to claim that I grasped it all in all its depths. No person of conscience would ever make such a claim. But I did work my way through the bulk of the received exegesis.

I found most of the commentaries prolix and absorbed by debates on exegesis, not by the sense of the passage at hand. Much of the commentary, moreover, concerns legal issues vivid only long after the Mishnah was published, so, as classicists have known since the Renaissance and Bible scholars since the time of Spinoza, to read an ancient text in light of its later exegesis is to commit anachronism.

True, no one proposes to ignore what other, earlier commentators have said about a given text. But, it seems, only in the subject at hand do we not only err but *sin* if we ask the text to form its own first, best commentary, as I did in my Mishnah-commentary.

X

Readers who have come this far will wonder, as I still wonder, why the heat, the nasty and the mean rhetoric, when all I want to know is what a text is and means. But the issues really do matter. I do not blame the other side for its anger. It proves they care. I care too, but it is about something else.

---

[7] Cf. my *History of the Mishnaic Law of Purities* (Leiden, 1974–1977) I–XXII. I covered the remainder of the Mishnah, the second through the fifth divisions, in another twenty-one volumes, and my former students completed the work for Mishnah and Tosefta Zeraim, the first division, in a sequence of monographs and dissertations. On the basis of this labor of infinite care about detail, I am declared "notoriously indifferent to detail." On the basis of occasional mistakes—to be regretted, to be corrected—work of genuine care, accurate over the vast majority of its details, is found "sloppy." No one can accuse the critics of an excessive concern to be meticulously fair.

I perceive the classical literature of Judaism as a great work of humanity. (As a religious Jew, I hasten to add, it is humanity responding to God's revelation.) We have in the writings of the ancient rabbis an amazing intellectual achievement. For what, in sum, they did was to search out the most profound layers of logic and order concealed in the superficial levels of triviality and nonsense. They took up much the same philosophical program as occupied other philosophers of their time, asking, for example, about the relationship between the potential and the actual, the acorn and the oak. They inquired about the power of human will to change the facts of life. They speculated about the nature of mixtures just as did the Stoic physicists and in exactly the same logical classifications and categories.

But our sages of blessed memory delivered their judgments not in engaging and accessible dialogues, as did Plato, nor even in response to the immediately accessible essays on virtue, the good life, and the ideal state essays we read today with pleasure, such as Aristotle wrote. Our sages spoke of things people really knew, could feel and touch, sweat and excrement, menstrual blood and the excretions of the sexual organs. They asked about mixtures of gravy and meat, of wool and linen. They taught theory only through example, and they drew example from commonplace and workaday realities. Out of all this they produced with extraordinary art a book of great poetry, the Mishnah, which also, properly read, turns out to be a book of great philosophy: an orderly and disciplined statement of the order and rule of life.

8. BEING JEWISH AND STUDYING ABOUT JUDAISM

I formulate in terms of Judaism the issue of descriptive and normative dimensions in the study of religions not because I am a Jew or only because I must talk about things I know. The reason is that, in general, discussions of the relationship between religion and religiosity and the academic study of religion, or between piety and the academic analysis of piety exhibit flaws of abstraction. Supposedly addressed to the generality of religions and conceived within the notion that piety is piety wherever it is found, these discussions actually homogenize all religions within the conceptual norms of Christian—and post-Christian—experience. They generalize on the basis of one very particular, if widespread, formulation of the question, never recognizing that the issue has been stated in a way distinctive to that one group alone. Many sorts of religions come under study, and diverse sorts of believers, sometime-believers, and non-believers engage in study. I therefore shall state matters in the context of a single, small, and unrepresentative religious group, those Jews who also are Judaists, people of Jewish origin who also believe in and practice Judaism. In doing so, the theological norms of a concrete and carefully delimited religious tradition may be permitted to illuminate the discussion, something they simply cannot do when under discussion is piety or religiosity in general.

My argument is in two parts. First I propose to take up an important criticism of the academic study of religion, the view that by insisting upon detachment and disengagement, we place an obstacle in the way of the understanding of religion. Students seeking religious knowledge for their own use do not find it in our classroom. The defense of the position that religions are to be described, not advocated, rests upon a theory of the limitations of the classroom. In the second part, I turn this theory into a critique of the descriptive study of religions. My point is that exactly the same limitations on the former position set the bounds for the latter. In point of fact both approaches to the study of religion— descriptive and normative—replicate a profound flaw in the humanities in general, a flaw which, I shall suggest, derives from the modes by which our minds grasp and respond to reality.

I

The academic study of religions in America and Canada, and more recently, in Britain, has developed a set of norms and convictions on the place of religiosity and individual belief in the classroom. We do not pray in classrooms. We do not advocate that students adopt belief in God, let alone specific theological positions. Our lectern is not confused with a pulpit. We do not preach. We teach. We do not teach religion, moreover, but we teach *about* religion, a distinction absolutely fundamental to our work. It goes without saying that we take as our principal responsibility the task of preserving objectivity about our subject, neutrality on its truth-claims. Scholarly standards of careful inquiry and dispassionate examination of facts are the norm. These convictions form the theory in virtually all departments of religious studies in universities and colleges, whether public or private, Church-related or secular. If they are subject to serious challenge, it is not in the paramount journals and scholarly societies devoted to the academic study of religions. To be sure, these principles set up a norm by which all, when measured, may for one infraction or another be found wanting. Their practical applications and their implications, moreover, remain subject to much deep thought. Honorable people disagree on the requirements for the academic approach to religion-study. But if there is disagreement on the principle that religion in the academic setting is to be studies with detachment and objectivity (however these words be interpreted), it is not public. It enjoys no powerful advocacy known to me.

Yet one commonplace criticism of the position just now outlined, stated crudely and often advanced by sectarians and advocated *pro domo*, is this: If Moses, Jesus, or Muhammed, let alone Confucius, Zoroaster, or Buddha, were to apply to your department, and if (in this truly eschatological moment), you actually had an opening, under no circumstances would you take seriously his application for a position. It is all right to teach about Jesus. But Jesus may not teach. On that basis you exclude believers and practitioners of faith. Twenty-five years ago the notion was widespread that believing Jews should teach what they believe as Jews, and so too with the varieties of Christians, with Moslems, Buddhists, and the like. Now, by contrast, you give preference to an attitude not merely of secularity and distance from the subject but of militant secularism. You do not give place to courses within religious belief, only courses about religious belief.

It is an evasion to reply that the classroom is not composed of members of a single church, so that advocacy and commitment leave no room for students who do not believe what is advocated (except that they convert). The pluralistic character of most universities is a fact, not a norm. It defines the context, but it cannot be asked to govern, or even to explain, what is done in context. It would, after all, be quite feasible to teach courses in Judaism for Jews, and courses in Judaism for non-Jews, and so with the other religions. It is not merely an evasion but deliberate fraud to claim that only people outside of a tradition, who cannot be suspected of advocacy thereof, are capable of scholarship and therefore of truly academic teaching about said tradition. The fact is that scholarship depends for its agendum, its definition of its task, upon social and cultural conditions. Scholars moreover study what interests them. A natural and perfectly legitimate criterion of interest is personal engagement.

If one is engaged by a subject, how is the subject not given the benefit of advocacy by its mere location at the top of the agendum of a course or department? Professors of Free Enterprise need not advocate free enterprise. By merely giving their courses, they cannot avoid placing into prominence, and therefore exposing the claims of, free enterprise. Advocacy is beside the point. In this regard the Soviets provide us with a fine model. They have institutes of religion *and atheism*, surely a fairer and more objective way of phrasing the agendum, if truth-claims of religion be at its top. I regard as false in fact and bigoted in spirit the claim that believers simply cannot engage in scholarship. If, therefore, we are not prepared to appoint Jesus or Moses, or people today who lay claim to do their work and embody their spirit and speak their message, the reason has to be made clear.

I wish now to restate the question as it is phrased by a colleague. After reading my lecture, *The New Setting for Jewish Learning: Towards a Theory of University Studies in Judaism* (above, Chapter 3), Professor Arthur Green, University of Pennsylvania, replied as follows:

> What I find disturbing about the university as a setting for most of Jewish studies in America is not so much its assimilatory character or its preference for the general over the particular, as its deep secularity. The conviction expressed in our curriculum seems to be that the sacred was an important part of human existence in primitive society, and perhaps survived right down to the eighteenth century. But it surely has nothing to do with contemporary existence. Given the uncomfortable relationship so many of our colleagues have with their own confessional backgrounds, departments of religious studies are the last places a truly searching student should go to learn about the religious life in any sort of personal way. I do not advocate missionizing. But I do wonder whether our highly self-conscious commitments to critical distance and objectivity do not do a disservice both to our students and to the subject we teach.

What I find pertinent in Green's observation is his question of whether we truly analyze and interpret the data of religion within the hermeneutical framework I outlined earlier. In the same letter, Green states an alternative worthy of serious thought: "A real commitment to the humanities must involve a search for wisdom and entails a kind of learning pertinent to personal growth and openness of mind. Our work suffers from the bifurcation of the search for wisdom from the quest for knowledge."

II

Our education and inclination prepare us to teach about this-worldly phenomena, the effects, of religion. We bring to the classroom the facts produced in this world. We then try to analyze those data in accord with th e worldly hermeneutic: the inner logic, the social meaning, the world-constructing power of myth, for example. The materials we study and teach bear other meanings. They claim to speak of another realm of reality, to know not only about this world, but also about the supernatural world and sacred things. We should need far more direct knowledge and experience of the world of the sacred to go in our teaching beyond the sole imminent facts of religion in this world. To analyze "sacred perspectives on the sacred," to view religion religiously, we should need a more complete grasp of how that other, transcendent world of the sacred is to be expressed in the utensils of language and concept, expressible (if not verifiable) experience. For so far as the classroom is not meant to be a place of religious experience and activity, it makes no room for such experience, but only the (admittedly antiseptic) analysis of such experience and its effects. The academic world is made of words, not supernatural experience. We do not sing, we do not pray, we do not meditate, we do not repeat sacred formulas, we do not fast, burn incense, dance or otherwise move or control our bodies and attain visions. All we do is talk and think.

Having completed the descriptive task which words permit, we simply are not able to replicate the experience of the religious life. Even if all the students were Jewish, not all of them have the capacity or will to enter into the religious life of Judaism. But even if they all perceived themselves as religiously Judaic, what academic purpose, for example, would be served by having them first analyze the formal and conceptual structure of the Jewish Prayerbook, then pray it? No one can claim that having done the analysis, we have said all there is to be said. We have, however, said all that we can and should say upon the basis of our own knowledge and experience.

But there is a second, still more powerful limitation to the possibilities of bringing into the study of religion the experience or practice thereof. The religious life, complex and subtle, does not begin here and now, but in a rich range of experiences of birth and upbringing. Religious experience rests upon prior experience of home and family, church, nation, and society. It cannot be realized, let alone replicated, in the classroom solely upon the basis of analysis of a book and its ideas. For example, prayer itself depends upon altogether too subtle a context: light, sound, gesture, the organization of space, the presence of sancta, adepts, and virtuosi. Jewish prayer depends upon dancing, music, and silence; it is physical, expressed through the body; it is intensely personal, yet collective. The prayers which are said evoke worlds not present. When we *daven*, we move through many ages and situations. Yet in the person of the individual and in the reconstitution of the sacred community, they are very much at hand. How dare we pray except in the congregation of Israel, before the Torah of Israel? Analysis of the ideas and structure of the Prayerbook does not facilitate prayer. It may not even be pertinent to praying. It is simply a small movement toward interpretation and understanding.

To recapitulate this part of the argument: In the classroom all we have is language of a particular kind to deal with an aspect of an experience of a distinctive sort. Language cannot wholly replicate and encompass, but can only diminish, the totality of the religious world of Judaism. We indeed use language suitable for description and analysis. That language cannot recreate the inner meanings and rich dimensions of the Judaic religious life. We distort and destroy those inner meanings if we pretend that they are to be replicated outside of life's disciplines, the everyday experience of history's meanings. The classroom, which is to say, the act of study by itself, is inadequate. Even if all students were Jewish and wished to become Judaic, in the university we cannot promise them what we cannot give: the authentic growing-into-Torah and reaching toward, responding to, God through Torah, which form the center of the Judaic life. This takes place in the setting of the this-worldly life and supernatural context of the Jewish people. One enters the Judaic situation solely by being raised a Jew or deliberately and in full consciousness turning toward Judaism. Nurture, whether from birth or from conversion, takes place in the life of encounter with life perceived and lived through the prism of Torah. It is in the streets and in the home. The intellectual side is subservient, even within the Judaic system, to the experience and construction of the world through the knowledge of Torah. Religiosity attained through nurture is not gained by academic inquiry.

The reason that we address the issue in terms particular to a single religious tradition should now be clear. The question takes its departure from a false conception of the theology and piety of Judaism, an inappropriate notion of what "expressing Judaism" or "personal engagement with Judaism" requires. Classroom advocacy of the truth-claims of Judaism, of acceptance of Judaism as one's religion, is irrelevant to Judaism because mere confession of the truth of the tradition is insufficient. Only by a whole and complete definition of one's way of life in terms of the discipline of Torah, entering into the common life of the sacred community of Israel, devoting one's life to the demands of Torah upon all modes and aspects of life and thereby submitting to God's will, does one enter into the Judaic framework. Too small a part of life takes place in the classroom. Too modest a portion of the intellect is engaged by the claims to truth subject, to begin with, to advocacy in class. Advocacy is irrelevant to what is advocated. To state matters simply: Judaism does not happen in a classroom, and to begin with it is not learned principally in books.

The issue in fact is phrased in terms of a religion which deems propositional advocacy to form the center of the religious life. Solely within such a notion of what being religious means does one confront the challenge of the "truly searching student who wishes to learn about the religious life in some sort of personal way." But I cannot think of any religion to which such a search pertains, other than a religion consisting wholly of philosophy. A philosophical religion expressing its world-view, constructing reality, and defining and shaping experience, entirely in terms of statements claimed to be of fact, does not exist. Religions exist in nominalist reality: churches, not religious institutions, Torah, not revelation, the God of Abraham, Isaac, and Jacob, or God the Father, the Son, and the Holy Spirit, not the divinity, Talmud Torah, not the study of facts about the Jews. True, we *talk about* religion, as though there were such a thing. But we *study* religions, concrete, specific things.

To conclude: Talmud Torah, the Hebrew words which signify study of the holy books, does not take place in a university classroom because Talmud Torah happens only in the community of Israel. It follows that what we do in the classroom is something quite different, even though the form—the act of study of books deemed by Judaism to be sacred and the processes of learning in them—is on the surface the same. What we do when we study religions is to be defined in its own terms. The classroom is incongruous to the religious quest. The holy community is the appropriate locus. The Judaic religious life in all details takes place within the setting of Israel, the holy community upon whom is set the mountain of Sinai. God without Israel is not the Lord (*hashshem*). Torah without God is not Torah. In religious context, Israel without Torah and God is nothing, a no-people. All elements of the triad define and delimit all others. To the tensions and inner stresses of the Judaic religious life, therefore of the quest for a point of entry into that religious life, the classroom is, in an exact sense of the word, *cosmically* irrelevant.

III

What do we legitimately undertake in the academic study of religion? We have now especially to confront the challenge of whether, and in what ways, what we do distorts the thing to which we do it, religions.

We do not distort something by describing some of its external traits. If I am able to explain to students some of the central symbolic and mythic structures of Judaism, to account for and clarify lines of their development through the ages, to demonstrate the complexity and subtlety of the tradition, so to call into question the possibility of defining as an *-ism* so diverse a corpus of phenomena, and yet to insist that definition is possible—if I can do these things, I have not taught the students something untrue to the subject. I have only not taught them everything true about the subject. The great methodologists of the academic study of religions have given us a dense agendum of questions to be brought to the data of the various religious traditions. In asking those questions, we do not inquire into all aspects of the diverse traditions. We interpret only those which impinge upon society and intellect, the shared imagination of the community of the faith, its capacity to shape the reality in which that community makes its life.

The whole truth of necessity eludes us. There are things we cannot know. Much which we do know we perceive only dimly and through a dirty mirror. But the delineation of the realm of knowledge marks out the frontier of ignorance: conceptual incapacity. The process of interpretation of things transcendent and the search for understanding of other, inner worlds begin and end in humility before the unknown. But the process and search do affirm that some things are to be understood in the immanent context of society and intellect.

In my view the claim that only the insider, the participant, is able to study and fully understand a religious tradition constitutes a polite statement of obscurantism. For who is the insider, and who is further inside the tradition than some other, to tell us when we have reached the inner precincts of the temple of belief? I know no keepers of the grail, no guardians of the sanctum of the faith, possessed of the ultimate authority over us all to say, "Yes, this indeed is Torah and what it truly means." The corpus of diverse opinions on all important questions within Judaism testifies against the certainty claimed in behalf of the insider. The insider furthermore is apt to lose all perspective on the whole. The participant is unlikely to perceive the interrelationships between one religious tradition and all others, to understand that most basic fact about religions, which is their context within humanity. Accordingly, what interpretation is possible, what understanding is to be promised, without perspective on the whole of a massive historical religious tradition, on the one side, and on its still larger context as religious phenomenon, on the other?

The academic description and interpretation of religions nonetheless do distort the data of religions. But this is in a different way. The distortion is in the very act of academic perception. For the classroom is a place of talk. Its capacity to replicate the reality to be subjected to interpretation depends upon words. Through the processes of the intellect we recreate the thing we wish to examine. We lay forth its traits, define its terms, describe its modes of functioning, then ask about its meaning within the hermeneutic disciplines at hand.

The obverse side of the critique of the criticism of the academic study of religion is at hand. Since we do not dance, or sing, or pray, burn incense, fast, or mumble sacred formulas, it follows that all we do do is try through words to lay forth what happens to those who do dance, pray, form transcendent community, interpret history, and thereby know God. The academic classroom by its nature and by definition effects a kind of subtle reductionism. Without intellectual articulation of their convictions intellectuals carry forward the belief that, through the intellect, reality is recreated and thereby subjected to interpretation. Our strength also is our weakness: our minds cannot but mislead us. In the study of religions in particular the act of learning begins in the reduction of religions to words. The misstep of learning is reductionism through intellectual reification.

What makes learning possible is the capacity to set into words things which are observed or experienced. What facilitates learning is the vast corpus of intellect produced within religions. For what we study is written texts, ideas, the language to which religions are committed. Yet the problem of correctly interpreting the holy books is exceedingly complex. For words are written down by someone, in some context. True, we may describe the person and the context. Yet words also continue to endure, take up a life of their own. The context changes, therefore meanings imputed to words change also. If, as I said, intellectuals maintain that through the intellect, they recreate and therefore interpret reality, then what is the reality laid forth by the words—the propositions of faith, the prayers, the stories—subjected to study? Is it that of the writer, or of a person who read and appropriated for his or her own life that which was written? Is it then a century, or two centuries, or a millennium after the text embarked on its journey through history? A central obstacle to the academic study of religions is the fact that religions change, and even though we accurately describe and interpret the world of a given religion at some one point in its history, that which we describe is not the totality of the religion under study. As intellectuals we construct systems. But the task of construction and interpretation is made rather complex by the fact that systems scarcely endure for a generation, while religions go on and on through time. This second aspect of the problematic of studying religions is now to be given appropriate emphasis. For my claim is not only that the intellect is insufficient to the replication of that which is studied. It also is that what the intellect is best able to do in this context, which is description and interpretation, is itself not congruent to that which is studied.

In the case of Judaism, for example, we have an exceptionally dense corpus of writings of intellectuals (intellectuals by definition) on the things which, through words, seem to them susceptible of inscription for transmission and study in the coming generations. It was their conviction that the study of the holy books they produced and handed on for transmission would succeed in evoking for the coming generations the truths set down in those holy books. They could come to such a conviction that writing things down is all right, specifically because they took for granted the words would be read in their very own context. Context is defined by both community and conviction. How could someone in fifty or a hundred years, living as I do and experiencing the world as I experience it, *not* precisely grasp the meaning of my words? But when those who do not stand within the context of the writers-down of words come to see those same words, how difficult is it to do so? In the academic study of religions, accordingly, deep calleth unto deep, the religious intellectuals, laying down the norms and meanings of their worlds in words, speak to the intellectuals who describe religions. By definition, the one is deprived of the power of speech, the other, of the power of hearing. In the academic study of religions, the dumb address the deaf. The dumb, to be sure, in general are dead. But the living deaf pretend to hear. There is no remedy to this grotesque dilemma, because the classroom simply cannot serve for the replication of life's full and rich context. Even if we danced, sang, burned incense, or spent our fifty minutes with our students reciting Psalms, even if all our students were Jews and we all were rabbis, we still should not have entered into the realities both interpreted and created by these merely-intellectual processes.

What impedes the authentically-*religious* study of religions in the classroom also presents an obstacle before the authentically-*academic* study of religions in the classroom. The changing reality we seek to describe and interpret is outside. We are inside. The reason is clear when we define that "we" who are inside. We are intellectuals, people who suppose that words will serve to create a context for the analysis and interpretation of reality. We take for granted the capacity of language and thought to correspond to reality. But the very statement of a thing obscures its character.

I offer for one evocative example what happened to me when I tried to define and describe cult in the setting of Israelite and Judaic religion of antiquity. I asked, "What is cult?"

The answer, "Sacrifice."

I: "True, but where is cult?"

The answer: "Temple."

"Fine," I said, "And what is Temple?"

"A place of cult."

"Splendid. And what happens in the cult?"

"Sacrifice."

This little colloquy left me with the uneasy sense that we had gotten nowhere, yet had used all the right words for the right things; there had been a true rectification of names. Then it occurred to me that the students had no visual perspective of sacrifice.

I began again. "A priest gets up in the morning. He comes to the Temple. What does he do first to 'engage in the cult'?"

Silence.

Finally the wheels begin to turn. "He washes up."

"Why does he wash up?"

Silence.

"Well, all right, he washes up. We'll talk about the reason later on. Then what does he do?"

"He *sacrifices*."

I (tearing my hair): "He does *what*?"

"He sacrifices."

"O.K.: *What* does he sacrifice? And what does he 'sacrifice' *with*?"

"He 'sacrifices' an animal, a sheep."

"Great. With what?"

There followed a long silence.

Finally, I: "How about a knife?"

After general agreement that you 'sacrifice' a sheep with a knife, I asked, "Then, in this context, *what* is sacrifice?"

"Taking a knife, taking a sheep, cutting the sheep's throat."

This step forward yielded the next question: "What happens then?"

It would be hopeless to list the answers—"the priest prays" "God is pleased" "everyone says psalms." No one proposed: "The sheep bleeds to death."

After I contributed that stunning fact, I asked, "What happens to the blood?"

And so it went.

In point of fact, the language I had used to approach this most central aspect of the Israelite and Judaic religious life, this "mode of service God," had in fact obscured the exact reality of what is done, what really happens. *Temple* bears no relevance to the known experience of the students. Does *butcher-shop*? "Sacrifice" in our setting is so elegant and elevated a word, so full of noble and spiritual nuance, as to have been deprived of its concrete and ordinary meaning. It hardly needs saying that, when I returned to the matter of "purification" from "uncleanness"—that is, "the priest washes up"—another very long process of freeing ourselves from the burden of the meanings associated with our everyday language had to begin. Words had led us to a reality both contained within and obscured by words. The work of learning can be done in some measure. It is a long and painful process, to which we have to subject ourselves to begin with, our students only afterward.

If it is generally agreed, therefore, that the study of religions appropriate to the classroom is the description and interpretation of religions, then I think the requirements of description have more fully to be realized and spelled out. For I do not conceive that the work cannot be done. I argue only that it presently is not much attained.

The reason is, first, our stress, in the generality of courses in religious studies, upon the intellectual analysis of the work of intellectuals. We pay disproportionate attention to issues of faith in theological and other intellectually accessible form. That of course is to succumb to the temptation of the classroom, to the one thing it is easy to do there.

Second, description through words, as I have tried to illustrate, is incomplete when we have not made certain we have fully analyzed the words we use against the evolving thing the words are supposed to contain, recreate, or evoke. The large words of religious studies speak of things done by people who are not professors, and who would not grasp the words which *we* apply to the things *they* do. That of course is of no consequence. But the students to whom we speak also take up our language without understanding that to which it refers, imitate us without understanding, just as we may well imitate our teachers, the books we read, without taking that additional step of imagining the thing at hand. Using "sacrifice" instead of "take a knife and cut a sheep's throat and collect the blood," to return to my example, facilitates intellectual reflection about vast and lofty things. It does not tell us in a concrete way exactly what happens, the thing about which we think.

If our being intellectuals stands in the way of our mind's work of description as much as it makes that work possible, the philosophical frame of mind within which our work is done limits our capacities at interpretation. For proper interpretation of religions requires the description of context, of the things which come before the thing we seek to interpret, the things which, round about it, form its setting, and those that come thereafter. Suitable description of religions requires us to set all things into relationship with all other things, sacrifice to Temple, priesthood, social caste, doctrine of atonement and sin, for example. If we capture these things all at once, as they balance with one another and form a whole house of meaning, we may begin to interpret and understand what holds the whole together, that ultimate point at which all things make sense. But the house of meaning is a house of cards. The cards themselves are cut-outs. When they form a house, it collapses, to be reconstructed in age succeeding age.

The movement and dynamism of religions require description over a long continuum, just as much as the static construct of religions is to be laid forth for some one moment. The histories of religions, not merely the phenomenon, the condition, of religions at some one moment in those histories, remain to be described. These histories, in my judgment, form the exegetical fulcrum for the interpretation of religions. Intellectuals' modes of thought are notoriously unable to cope with change. Endings and beginnings are disorderly. Systems are susceptible to philosophical description and analysis only when in their middle, stable stages. But the modes of thought of historians commit exactly the sort of reductionism for which, I have tried to suggest, philosophers bear guilt. For to them there are no systems, no worlds of meaning, but only sequences of ways in which for a moment things happen to fall together. The philosopher in the guise of anthropologist seeks to define and describe taxonomies of systems. The philosopher in the guise of historian asks for hermeneutic guidance on how these sorts of systems interrelate, how one dialectically arises from the last and generates the next. It follows that the work of description and interpretation is deeply flawed, both because the thing described and interpreted comes to us from intellectuals, and because we ourselves are intellectuals.

IV

The dilemma of religious studies is authentic to the character of its subject: religion. The nature of religions is to be traditional. As Jonathan Z. Smith states, "Regardless of whether we are studying texts from literature or non-literate cultures, we are dealing with historical processes of reinterpretation, with tradition. . . . For a given group at a given time to choose this or that mode of interpreting their tradition is to opt for a particular way of relating themselves to their historical past and social present." All religions which last for more than moment have therefore to confront the dilemma of continuity, to find a way either to legitimate change or to obviate its meanings. *The way is through interpretation, in a synchronic framework, of the diachronic facts of faith.* And whether the expression of interpretation be through philosophy, theology, history, or myth, the task is invariably one and the same.

The dilemma of our work is elegantly captured in a myth of Talmudic Judaism, which for its part must find a way of bringing into relationship with the Written Scriptures the rich and diverse developments of the Judaic religious life over the many centuries since Scripture. I quote the story at some length because it states, in its own way, the problem of continuity in religion, therefore giving concrete expression to the dilemma of students of religion: What is it that is subjected to description and interpretation? (Happily, the story also permits us to account for our unwillingness to appoint Moses to the faculty of Religious Studies in the area of Judaism.) It is found in Babylonian Talmud, Menahot 29b:

> Rab Judah said in the name of Rab:
> A. When Moses ascended on high, he found the Holy One, blessed be He, engaged in affixing coronets to the letters [of the Torah, that is, putting three small strokes on the top of various Hebrew letters in the form of a crown].
> Moses said, "Lord of the universe, who stays they hand? [That is, is there anything lacking in the Torah, that these additions to the letters in which the Torah is written have to be added]?" He answered, "There will arise a man, at the end of many generations, by the name of Aqiva b. Joseph. He will expound upon each tittle heaps and heaps of laws."

"Lord of the Universe," Moses said, "Let me go and see him."

He replied, "Turn around."

[Moses then is transported to the academy of 'Aqiva's disciples, and he listened to the discourses upon the law]. He was not able to follow the arguments or to understand what was said. He became ill at ease. But when they came to a certain subject, the disciples said to the master, "How do you know it?"

Aqiva replied, "It is a law given to Moses at Sinai."

Moses then was comforted.

B. Moses then returned to the Holy One, blessed be He, and said, "Lord of the universe. You have such a man—and yet you give the Torah through me!" He replied, "Be silent, for such is My decree."

Then Moses said, "Lord of the universe. You have shown me his Torah. Now show me his reward."

"Turn around," said God. Moses turned around and saw people weighing out the flesh of Aqiva at the butcher shops [for Aqiva is believed to have died as a martyr in the time of the Bar Kokhba war, and his skin was flayed from his body].

"Lord of the universe," cried Moses, "Is such Torah and such the reward for Torah?!"

"Be silent," God replied, "for such is My decree."

The second part of the story (B) introduces a highly dissonant element, since, to begin with, the issue of the reward of Aqiva is hardly required by the issue of the story at the outset. Had the tale ended with the comforting of Moses, it would have been complete and wholly satisfactory.

The issue, it is clear, is the accommodation of change to the condition of a continuous religion which claims to be perfect, therefore unchanging. The central claim of Judaism is to be continuous with Sinai, just as a principal concern of Christianity has been to establish its continuity with the Old Testament. The problem to be solved by the Judaic thinkers is not so easily solved as that facing the Christian ones. The latter claim that Torah is fulfilled at the end, in Christ. The former for obvious reasons can lay no equivalent claim in behalf of Moses, and therefore turn the matter on its head. The continuity is projected at the outset, not at the end. The Oral Torah is present at th e beginning of the Written one. Everything which the greatest master of the Oral Torah would say already had been said by the great authority of the Written one.

In historical context, the story assigned to Rab, an authority of the third century, deals with and expresses an opinion on the claim, laid forth in behalf of Mishnah, to be Torah. Mishnah, a vast code put together toward the end of the second century, is set before the people of Israel as God's will, as Torah to be kept by the Jews. Yet Mishnah's laws are assigned to first and second century authorities, who rarely purport to base their views upon Scripture, to reach their opinions through exegesis of the Written Torah. The Oral Torah therefore is subject to criticism of two kinds. First, its claim to give law upon the foundation of reason, rather than Scriptural exegesis, is challenged (in Sifra, for instance). Second, its claim to be Torah is made to depend, as in the present story, upon its relationship to Mosaic revelation, which is to say, if Moses had not already said it, then Aqiva could not be believed.

But of course the critique also contains within itself a formidable defense. Mishnah indeed does depend upon exegesis. Moses truly did say what the latter-day authority, Aqiva, without citing Mosaic revelation, also says. The tradition is continuous. The continuity consists—so it is claimed—in the unfolding of the inner logic of the law, the discovery, by later generations, of meanings logically implicit in the words of earlier ones. The whole, of course, testifies to the deeply intellectual character of the people who to begin with ask the question and find the answer. For it is they who perceive the discontinuity to begin with. The intellectuals find themselves constrained to ask the historical question of data which, to begin with, are meant to construct an enduring reality, not subject to history. Had the story ended with Moses' being comforted, we should have concluded with this observation: The inner dynamic of Judaism, its capacity both to respond to the changing circumstances of history and to accommodate the effects of change within its enduring, unchanging world of meaning, corresponds to, is replicated by, the dilemma of the academic study of religion.

For the limited capacities of intellectuals studying religion begin in the use of language for the purpose of study, both to contain and to create reality. And reality cannot, in the nature of things, find whole and permanent place within language. Language best serves to give unchanging names to things which are supposed to remain always the same. It is suited to the one-time rectification of names. But the names it gives obscure the changing things which are named, place over them a veil by which the intellect both grasps and misunderstands that which is subject to thought, the thing beyond. The naming of things generates the forming of systems and structures of names. These, in the nature of things, must be static and unchanging, for structures or systems serve only so long as they stand still and remain in balance. A system which changes in even one of its constituents changes in them all. The system then described is no longer the system which has been described.

A taxonomy of systems will not serve, unless the processes by which one system yields the next and derives from the last, accommodates new elements and sloughs off old ones, are both documented and then themselves systemically described. If all that endures, in the work of studying religions, is an account of the dynamics of change, then religion is described as it never has been experienced, solely as a process of becoming, but not as a state of being, understanding, and enduring. And yet, we should have concluded, the central dilemmas of our work accurately correspond to and replicate the character of the data which are subject to our descriptive and interpretative labor. In that wry and ironic fact is to be located the apologia for the infirmities and incapacities of our intellect: in mind we indeed do construct flawed reality outside.

Yet the story does not end with Moses' being comforted. It raises two dissonant notes, neither of them within the original melody. We cannot expect the question, Why is more Torah needed? to be followed by, Why is *Moses* needed? And had the story ended there, it still would have been complete. When then ask, "You have shown me his Torah, Now show me his reward"? The first of the two notes strikes a dissident chord, and so does the second. Still more disconcerting is the story's twin-response: "Be silent." "That is how I want things." Why ask a question, if you have no answer to it?

We surely cannot deem the story apologetic or place it into the category of didactic tales either. "Why Moses and not Aqiva? Because God wants it that way"—*cui bono*? For whom is such a question deeply relevant. "Why a reward of martyrdom? Because God wants it that way"— *cui bono*? To whom is the question of reward compelling? Why the way of martyrdom at the end? In the context of what I think is the shallow apologetic for Judaism constructed by nineteenth- and twentieth-century philosophers of Judaism, the one thing we should not have anticipated is invocation of silence before the unreasonable divine decree. We should find that Moses is preferable to Aqiva because—with diverse, rationalist answers given to complete the thought. Martyrdom will be set into the context of Israel's suffering; we shall hear about Job; and the story will be inserted whole into a homogenized mixture of homilies.

But that is not what happens in Rab Judah's report of Rab's story. In all its specificity and concreteness, the story speaks for, and to, someone. To whom is the question important: Why Moses and not Aqiva? To whom, if not the person who identifies with Aqiva and wants to find justification for his participation in the creation and revelation of the Torah of Moses. Why Moses and not *me*—since since I self-evidently discover truth not stated by Moses (if, to be sure, to be located within the words Moses did say)? The answer, I think, is self-evident once the question is asked as I have asked it. The question troubles the intellectual who sees his own contribution to be one of worth, yet who also is constrained to locate that contribution within the processes of tradition. It is a question for the schools. Moses, not you, because God wants it that way. And if you ask, why me, and not Moses, the answer is the same. The processes of mind are subject to God's will. God made the mind, you use it. And the matter of reward need hardly detain us. For who can deem self-evident a tie between the achievement of the intellect and the reward of this world? Who if not the intellectual? In a time of martyrdom, why should Aqiva *not* be martyred? Why is it not obvious that Torah invokes no privilege within the community of Israel? Learning does not invest the learner in a cloak of immunity from the condition of Israel as a whole. Such is the divine decree: Be silent.

V

It is difficult to imagine a more just punishment of intellectuals than the penalty of silence. To be told that, at some points, in response to some questions, the answer is found in silence is to invoke the notion that truth is found in what is whole, in the completion and complementarity of opposites. The work of intellectuals is conducted in words. Their thought, which is their being, is to give form through speech not only to thought itself but to the thing to which thought is devoted. We remind ourselves, therefore, that just as the whole consists of both speech and silence, just as speech is only one side of the unity of which the other side is silence, so our whole work consists of opposites.

The one side is the *hubris* of thinking that we may know and grasp things. The other is the *humility* of admitting the limitations of thought itself. The one side is the exclusion of Moses from our faculty because we do not need him. The other is the devotion of the faculty to the study of the one we do not need, even to the exclusion of the Torah of the one who engages in that study. We argue that the classroom is not a suitable place for the expression and practice of religion. For the same good and substantive reasons it also is not a wholly satisfactory locus for study *about* religion.

Critical distance and objectivity do not do disservice to religions about which we teach. It is our own frailty: the incapacity of mind, the distortion effected by learning, therefore teaching. This, I believe, captures the paradox in which we make our being, the ineffable tragedy of mind's incapacity to do its work, to grasp the human condition. For the mind too is mortal. In thought about itself, mind cannot transcend its own participation within the human condition. We cannot be more than what we are. That is why God tells us, through death, to be silent: Ask no more, risk no more, think no more.

Part Four

SCHOLARSHIP IN THE CONTEXT OF JUDAISM

9. TAKING THINGS APART TO SEE HOW THEY WORK

A long time ago, when I was a boy in West Hartford, I framed two fundamental traits that have never changed for me. First, I had to see for myself. Second, I liked to take things apart and to try to put them together again to see how they work. Whether it is a toy car or a system of Judaism, it would always be the same: on that my mind has never changed. As a boy I loved learning things, finding nearly everything interesting, nearly everybody with a story to tell. That is why I chose as my life trying to see for myself how Judaism worked, learning things about nearly everything in the interest in that one thing: on that my mind has never changed. I want to see how diverse groups of Jews worked out that way of life and that world view that framed their world. I want to know what it is about us as human beings that we learn from them, I mean, how, in the mirror of their world, we see some slight detail of ourselves, I mean, of us as humanity, as we are in God's likeness, in God's image. On that my mind will never change: we are in the likeness, we are in the image.

But on most other things, in the nature of things, my mind changes every day, and why not? For to reflect and reconsider is a mark of learning and growth, a measure of curiosity and intellectual capacity. For us who spend our lives as teachers and learners in the realm of religion in the here and now, to reach a firm and final "position" means to die, to stop our quest. For our subject lives, changes, grows. If, both in books and in the faces of the day we search for the record of God's image and God's likeness, then we can never finally master all the data or reach a firm conviction, short of knowing everything about everything and understanding it all, once for all.

I will be forgiven, therefore, if in the small and remote corner of the world in which I conduct my quest for what it means to be a human being, I seek, and find, new things from day to day. To say how my mind has changed is to catalogue all the things I have learned, specifying what is worth remembering, what forgetting, as well. My career, that is to say, my education in the study of Judaism, goes back to 1954, when I became a beginning student at the Jewish Theological Seminary of America. Happily for oratorical purposes, it divides into three periods, each of a decade, the historical, the literary, and the cultural. I work on the Talmud and related literature.

In my historical period, into the 1960s, I wanted to know what happened in the *time* of the Talmud.

In my literary period, into the 1970s, I wanted to know what happened in the *pages* of the Talmud.

In my cultural period, into the 1980s, I wanted to know what happened because of what is *said* in the Talmud.

So for a decade I worked on the Talmud and related writings as a historical source, for another decade I worked on the Talmud as a literary problem, and in the present period I work on the Talmud as a statement of culture, as an artifact of human expression, as a solution to someone's problem. For thirty years my mind remained constant that in hand we have, first, the record of a remarkable experiment in being human, hence a historical record, second, a complex and subtle experiment in recording, through *how* things are said as much as through what is said, the things people have learned from their experiment, hence, a literary monument. But, third and most important, there is something still more immediate. For what makes the Talmud and related literature not only interesting but also important for contemporary discourse on the human situation is not its historical facts or literary presence. If only Jews searching for their own heritage studied the Talmud as a work of law and theology, history and literature, or as a labor of faith and devotion to God's word, as Jews do study the Talmud in these dimensions, the rest of humanity would lose out on a small but valued part of the treasury of human experience. It is the testimony of the Talmud and related literature on a common human problem that we then should press.

Let me explain. When we consider the human situation of those Jews whose history and literature, whose law and theology, we have at hand, we understand the critical importance of that third dimension, that third decade—the 1980s—of my own life as a scholar, the dimension of the Talmud as a social construct, as a statement, beyond itself and its details, of a transcendent, larger whole. But who can hear it all, and all at once? The genius of a composer is to draw together many voices and enable them not only to speak all at once, which is mere cacophony, but to speak simultaneously and yet intelligibly and harmoniously, which is music, opera for instance. What composer can draw together so vast a literature, so diverse a set of themes and motifs, and form the whole into a whole? That, phrased in the language of music we all share, is the problem of my labor. Is it any wonder that, as I said at the outset, my mind should change and change and change? But if I am to be judged, as we all must be judged if we propose to do things without lives, then let me be condemned if I waste my opportunities, or let me be exonerated if I have freely exercised my powers of imagination and used my strength to grasp the whole and hold it all in balance and proportion, if I have shown imagination and capacity.

Let me then spell out this matter of imagination: what is wrong with reading the Talmud and related literature as only a historical record, as only a literary monument? And what is right about listening for its statement of culture and seeing it as an artifact of humanity faced with a particular problem? To do so I want to ask you to think not about ancient Israel, in the aftermath of a catastrophe of defeat, ancient Israel no longer in control of its land and of its life, ancient Israel facing a world less hospitable than any it had ever known. Rather I want to speak of Wales after Edward, Scotland after 1745 and of Ireland after Cromwell, after England. I swim every day with a sculptor of Canadian-Scottish origin. He explained to me why the Scots in Canada—at least, his family—will not plant Sweet William in their gardens and wear a black arm-band on the 16th of April. After nearly two and a half centuries and two nations later, the Scots remain defeated, beleaguered, out of kilter. Some people here may have followed the Masterpiece Theater performance of "To serve them all our days," and may recall that the Welsh hero, in an English public school, tells the headmaster that he cannot make it in England because he is "of the wrong nationality," and tells his girl-friend that the castles on the English-Welsh border are there to keep out "his" ancestors. The Welsh have not had their own nation for nearly seven centuries. But in mind they are Israel beyond catastrophe. And who needs to be reminded of the suffering of the Irish, whose history rivals that of us Jews for its pathos—and also, its resentment and its sense of long-nursed righteous grievance. I could not watch the end of the TV history of Ireland, any more than I could watch TV portrayals of the murder of the Jews of Europe. I cannot distinguish among those events that fall into the classification of "holocaust," to use the prevailing language-symbol. This digression carries us far from a meeting to talk about biblical and related studies, but it is important in explaining why I see the Talmud and related literature as a worthy object of today's imagination. It is worth trying to grasp the whole and hold it all in balance, because only in that way shall we be able to see the humanity in the circumstance preserved in those difficult and contentious writings, and only in that way shall we gain access to that distinctive version of a human experience common to us all. I mean defeat, disappointment, resentment, but also of renewal and sanctification.

That is why, to state matters briefly, I changed my mind about the value of historical inquiry by itself, and rejected the self-evidence of the worth of literary inquiry by itself. But I affirm them both in a larger search for meaning, for insight resting upon learning. We have to know what really happened, what came first and what took place next. The sources at hand, however, will stand in judgment on our work and find it insufficient, if that is all we want to ask them. For they have *more* to tell us. But, I think most of us now realize, they also have much *less* to tell us. The Talmud and related literature do not come to us from the hand of trained reporters, with tape recorders and video-cameras, and people have to read these sources in the same critical spirit that guides their reading of the Hebrew Scripture and the New Testament and much else. The first ten years of my life, marked by the *Life of Yohanan ben Zakkai* and the *History of the Jews in Babylonia*, marked off a long struggle to emerge from fundamentalist reading of rabbinic tales and stories, on the one side, and fundamentalist description of the life and culture of the Jews of that age, on the other.

I thought that if we could show *how* the sources work, we could gain accurate access at their historical records. That is why, in the next ten years, I took up problems of literary criticism, involving, in particular, the familiar and routine methods of form-analysis, redaction-criticism, dissection and reconstruction, and, in all, of an acerbic and cool encounter. The decade at hand—the 1970s—marked the transition that is critical to the future. I began the literary work with an interest in problems of a historical character, which I proposed to investigate through a critical reading of the diverse sources generally alleged to give information about those problems. To take my three studies, they involved a first century rabbi—Yohanan ben Zakkai revisited, then the Pharisees before 70, and finally, a critical figure in the age of reconstruction after the destruction of the Temple in A.D. 70, Eliezer ben Hyrcanus. In all three cases I wanted to read the sources critically, as they had not been read, essentially so as to produce answers to historical questions, such as had been answered many times before. The method was new to its field (but only to that field). But the program was very old and familiar indeed. That was the first half of the decade, from the late 1960s to the middle 1970s. But, alas, minds change. I continued the literary work with an interest in problems of a cultural and anthropological character.

To unpack this shift: throughout the work at hand—under way for fifteen years from 1960 to 1975—I faced the growing sense that everything I was doing was beside the point of the sources. By the mid-1970s, I realized that the questions were mine, but not theirs. Now my Orthodox Jewish friends always had told me so, since they thought history irrelevant (they called it, the story of what a rabbi had for lunch, not the story of what he stood for). They thought critical literary methods either heretical or old-hat (I never could tell which). But the questions of my Orthodox Jewish friends were those of the text. They asked little of interest in our own day. What I needed to find would be questions that were my questions, but questions also congruent to the answers that the texts provided in their ancient day. To move forward, in the same decade, in the late 1970s, I shifted my program. I wanted still to read the sources critically as literature, and I wanted still to come up with historical answers, I mean, a picture of how things were, not merely how the text portrays them. But what questions, what answers? I determined to ask the texts to tell me what they wanted to discuss, rather than what interested me. That meant to ask the Mishnah to be the Mishnah, the Tosefta, its supplement, to speak in its terms and along its own lines, so too the two Talmuds and the more important collections of exegeses of Scripture ("midrashim").

The present decade, the 1980s, for me is the age in which I am trying to describe the documents one by one but each one whole. I have thus far addressed the Mishnah as a whole and in its components, in my *Judaism: The Evidence of the Mishnah*, in that same exercise dealing also with the Tosefta. I have completed my first soundings in the Talmud of the Land of Israel, with the results in the paired works, *The Talmud of the Land of Israel*. Vol. 35. *Introduction. Taxonomy*, and *Judaism in Society: The Evidence of the Yerushalmi*, and I have dealt at some length with one collection of scriptural exegeses and asked how the framers of that collection appear to have thought they made a cogent and intelligible statement. This work is in *Judaism and Scripture: The Evidence of Leviticus Rabbah*. My present work takes up the same issues for the Babylonian Talmud. It is *Judaism in Conclusion. The Evidence of the Bavli*. Essentially, therefore, I have reached that point that, in my childhood, I would reach when I had taken the toy car apart and laid out all its bits and pieces.

No one will be surprised to know that it is harder to put things together than it is to take them apart. In three works I have tried to follow the familiar path of working on a particular problem, this time along a route dictated by the character of the documents at hand. Exploiting the earlier results of the description of documents one by one, and each one whole, I asked about the three fundamental questions of description of any religious system: revelation and canon, teleology and eschatology, and generative symbol. The works that have come out are *Midrash in Context. Exegesis in Formative Judaism, Messiah in Context. Israel's History and Destiny in Formative Judaism*, and *Torah: From Scroll to Symbol in Formative Judaism*. Clearly the third decade is nearly over.

What lies before is that ultimate question of childhood: how does it really work? Once, as I said, we have taken the car apart and seen how it is made up, can we put it together again? Just where and why and how did the system work, I mean, that system of Judaism created by the ancient rabbis and attested in their writings? To state matters somewhat differently, we know that the documents at hand fall into a single context, namely, that of the ancient rabbis. We also know that they come in a single classification, namely (for ancient times) (A) Jewish, and (B) rabbinical, writings. We know, more important, that the ancient documents are represented in various ways as being connected to one another. They not only fit together in one classification, but they also join together in one or another within that classification. The real question before us is not one of classification or connectedness, therefore, but rather, one of continuity. Are these texts continuous, and if so, what moves from one to the next and how does the movement take place? How do the diverse documents constitute one "Judaism"? True, in the eye of faith all of the documents at hand form a single statement, one of "Judaism," or, in the language of the faith, of "Torah." But that conviction forms a datum of the contemporary faith, not an analytical or categorical postulate. No one present thinks otherwise, unless you also regard the deepest conviction that there is one holy Catholic church, a single Christianity, a "church that is one in Christ"—unless you regard those profound Christian affirmations as serviceable descriptions of the this worldly history and character of Christian churches. So too with "Judaism" or "Torah"—let the work begin.

10. MY METHODS FOR THE THE STUDY OF RELIGION

When we seek to understand religion, two tasks demand immediate attention. We have, first, to specify what we wish to know about religion. We must, second, explain how we shall know when we are right and how we can tell when we are wrong in conclusions we propose about religion. With out a clear statement on both of these matters, we shall continue that endless exercise of hunting and gathering, selecting and arranging, that now serves many as theory of, and method for, the study of religion. That is to say, the generality of researches scarcely reaches that level of self-awareness that requires a statement of what, exactly, we wish to know. The larger number of books rarely contains an explanation of how we may claim to know right from wrong. The result is an endless gathering of information, the hunting-and-gathering stage of learning, and the aimless presentation of information that falls into the capacious space of show-and-tell we dignify as ethnography. Purposeful inquiry and rigorous reasoning transform what is now hunting and gathering into the quest for understanding, on the one side, and turn what is now the childhood pastime of show and tell into reasoned presentation of significant theories and theses, on the other. So, in a word, what we have constantly to explain about our work is precisely what we wish to know and exactly how we shall know when we have found it out.

These rather pragmatic and down-to-earth criteria for scholarly worth leave ample place for the theorizing about religion and for abstract discussion of methods for the study of religion. But from my perspective they also do define that part of the larger realm of theory that makes its impact upon the actual practice of the study of religion. For if I can tell you what I want to know and why, then I may also know how to design concrete and attainable projects of research. And if I can explain to myself how to tell right from wrong in the this-worldly quest for accurate information and defensible explanation, then I can carry out projects of research in full confidence of reaching results (whether positive or negative, things proved, things shown wrong or beyond proof) to share with others.

These same criteria—clear statements of what we want to know and how we shall know when we know it—also permit us to learn from *others*, not only from our own researches. For when I have a clear grasp of what another scholar wishes to tell me and why, and how that other scholar knows right from wrong, I can draw the necessary connections. I can build the required bridges, from here to there, even produce the illuminating analogies and metaphors, so I can grasp the work of that other scholar in all of *its* detail and complexity. The alternative—I mean, the failure to make an explicit statement of the scholarly program and method, the theory and the mode of inquire—I just now claimed produces at least the labor of hunting and gathering, the exercise of selecting and arranging for the purposes of show-and-tell. Why is that not enough? Because without metaphors and relationships none of us learn from the work of scholars who hunt and gather in some field other than our own. Why not? Because it is exceedingly difficult to read ethnography, including ethnography of religion, without discovering early on that we are learning a good bit more than we wish to know about the subject at hand. Too much is a mark of not enough, specifically, of insufficient explanation. Scholars who play show-and-tell end up talking mainly to a small in-group, and whether it is a group made of co-religionists or one composed of co-conspirators of an academic politics makes no difference. For information without purpose, inquiry without public and communicable results—these mark the parochial scholars, the ones who speak only to their own kind at first, and in the end, talk only to themselves. Self-absorption and narcissism may mark neurosis in the world at large, but they characterize the generality of scholarship in the academic realm. Theory and method present the indicated therapy.

What then do I wish to know, and how do I go about learning it? What I want to know is what from my youth I have always wanted to know, which is how religion relates to the social life of communities, and how the ideas that people hold relate to the world in which they live, or which they propose to create for themselves. These questions concern one aspect of religion, religion as a social force and a critical power in the formation of culture and imagination. They obviously do not exhaust what all of us wish to know about religion . But they do define one cogent program of learning. I need hardly point to the scholars, dead and alive, who have taught me the urgency of posing just these questions and modes of finding answers to them. They are not only represented by the names of Weber and Durkheim, Leach, Turner, Fernandez, Perry, and Douglas. They also are invoked by the names of Isaiah, Jeremiah, Ezekiel, not the mention the astounding framers of the pentateuchal traditions into what became, in Ezra's time, the Torah, or the founders of Judaism in the Talmudic canon. Nor would the founders and framers of the Christian Church who thought deeply about the city of God and the city of man regard as alien this central inquiry. We human beings are political animals. Religion has nearly always defined the political perimeters of the polis; of the nation and the community; of the holy people, Israel, and the Church, the body of Christ. So let us know what religion is as a social fact and a cultural force. That collective and social dimension does not measure all that religion is, but it surely defines one critical dimension.

If that is what I wish to know, in the modest realm of Judaism, then how do I find out? The answer derives from the character of the data at hand. I work on the formative period of Judaism. I ask why the form of Judaism that took shape in late antiquity (the Talmudic or rabbinic form, to use the adjectives supplied by the principal document and the honorific title of the principal hero of the faith) served when it did and flourished when it did. Why, also, and how did that same form of Judaism cease to serve where and whom and when it did and so in specific times and places how did it lose that quality of self-evidence that had long sustained Israel, the Jewish people.

What data I have in hand for late antiquity derive from the founders and the framers, and the data consists of a sizable and essentially cogent set of writings. I study not a religion but a library. This I propose to transform into the data of a religion. That is to say, I want to know whether the library at hand forms a mere collection of books, or constitutes a cogent canon, the literary expression of the world-view and way of life we know as the religious system, Judaism.

So I know about not the social life of an entire nation but the imaginative and intellectual life of a small group. I want to know how that vision—the fantasy of a handful of intellectuals—came to shape the perceptions of people everywhere, I mean nearly the whole of the Jewish nation, where ever they lived. I can describe, analyze, and interpret a single form of Judaism. I want to know how that Judaism succeeded while other Judaisms did not. I seek a theory of interpretation, one framed in relationship to the deepest and most dense layers of social meaning to which Jews responded—if in superficial detail, yet always cogently. What I wish to interpret is why this particular set of ideas turned out to serve the social group that held them and accepted the leadership of those who expounded them, and why other sets of ideas did not. I ask why a set of ideas of the type or character of the set at hand, I mean, the Judaism that served so long and well, proved self-evident to a group of the type or character of the group under study. Clearly, I therefore take a keen interest in the comparison of one construction of ideas, in one social setting, to another such construction, in a different social setting. And these societies self-evidently permit comparison and contrast in the two dimensions of our inquiry, the synchronic but also the diachronic. It is, therefore, a formidable program.

I do not mean to close without reference to how I shall know whether I am right and where I am wrong. Obviously, where work is underway and a theory is as yet in progress, we may postpone answering the question of falsification and verification. But where work is done or nearly so, we have to confront that painful question. I will allege that I have finished some things. I do have clear ideas. I do make concrete claims to describe, analyze, and interpret phases in the history of the formation of the Judaism under study and important components of the larger evidence, the larger literary canon that constitutes the data, for that Judaism. But if I have said what I think a document is and why I think it exhibits the traits that it exhibits and not some other traits, I have yet to frame that theory that ultimately will become susceptible to the test of falsification and verification. Why not? Because the ultimate test cannot derive from one system, or to state matters in a language different from the one we ordina rily use, no theory of explanation can posit that $N = 1.0$. So I shall know right from wrong, in the description, analysis, and interpretation of the formation of Judaism, only when I can compare what I think is so with what others think is so in the description, analysis, and interpretation of a Judaism different from the one at hand. All the more so, I must compare what I say about this kind of Judaism with what is to be said to interpret a religious formation or a religious tradition other than one that bears the adjective Judaic or falls into the classification of Judaisms. Until we gain that level of comparison, we work with mysteries. We describe with no perspective of depth and dimension. We analyze with no insight into what sustains a cogent structure. We interpret with no guidance other than plausible guesses. So the generation to follow will have an interesting task for itself.

11. AN INTERVIEW
by William Novak

So what are you working on these days?

I'm involved in a big project on the Babylonian Talmud. I'm trying to examine the text to see whether it's possible to describe the mentality of its authors. What I want to know is, what can we learn about the world-view of the people who made these statements?

Is this what you mean when you speak of moving from text to context?

Yes. I want to know why people say things in a certain way and not in some other way. It's really a question of style, because the Talmud is an enormously stylized document. How do you translate aesthetics and rhetoric—rituals of language—into cultural data? When you're dealing with questions of word choice and the arrangements of words, the Talmud lets you know that this stuff is vital. The speakers are always asking: "Why does he say it this way and not that way?" The assumption, which is absolutely valid, is that the speakers were vitally concerned with issues of aesthetics and rhetoric.

And what about the meaning of words?

That's something I don't work on. That's been done for a hundred years or more, and for most texts what we have is sufficient. Instead, I work on questions that have been ignored, questions of aesthetics and rhetoric, problems of description and interpretation of the whole document. Look: you and I express ourselves through sentences with a certain cogency. We argue propositions based on a shared logic that is basic to our culture. That's how we communicate. These people did too. Those are the aspects of a document that lead you into the worldview of the people who wrote it.

It almost sounds as though you don't want to get too close to the text.

You have to strike a balance. If you're too close to the text, you become an authority not *about* the text but *of* the text. You end up repeating what the text says, but in your own words.

So there has to be perspective and critical autonomy. On the other hand, you can have too much of a good thing. If you're too far from the text, it all dissolves into generalities. If you're standing up on a mountain, everything below looks pretty much the same.

I see the secular and humanistic study of religious texts as a three-part process. First we translate the text. Second, we determine its context: when was it written? how is it argued? Who was it written for? What is the system of logic it uses? Finally, we make generalizations about the text: we compare that world to other worlds, including our own, as we try to understand those people in terms of what we know about ourselves.

That's the pattern of my work. And I'm trying to come up with a theory of each major document, each text. They're always treated as a collection of homogeneous documents with everybody saying the same thing to everybody else, and that's just not true

As when people say "As we read in the Talmud..."

Not even that. As in *"The* Rabbis say . . ." But the texts aren't all the same. When I worked on Leviticus Rabbah (a fifth-century set of discourses built on some verses of Leviticus), for example, I discovered that it wasn't just a matter of commenting on verses of Scripture. It's true that the rhetoric of Leviticus Rabbah is a rhetoric of exegesis. But the logic is not a logic of exegesis at all. Through their citations of verses, they're really *saying* things.

Previously, the things people wanted to say were attached to specific texts. In Genesis Rabbah, for example, you get straight exegesis. They comment on this verse, they comment on that verse. In the later collections, they're much more discursive. But Leviticus Rabbah stands at the turning point between straight exegesis and the kind of straight discursiveness we find in the Pesiqtas. It's a point of tension, which makes it very revealing. They are trying to speak discursively while remaining within the framework of exegetical discourse.

I gather you weren't always approaching the text on this level. Does this approach represent a shift in your methodology?

To some extent, yes. The shift came around 1970. I had written *A History of the Jews of Babylonia*. In the prefaces to volumes 3, 4, and 5 I signalled that I was unhappy with the existing methods, which were credulous and gullible, but that the questions as I then framed them permitted me to work this way.

In view of the methods I use now, that *History* is a mere curiosity. But it's been accepted into the scholarly canon. I see it quoted, even in those circles which reject the rest of my work.

I want to talk about those circles in a moment. But first, where did your shift occur?

In 1970, when I published *Development of a Legend*.

That was about Yohanan ben Zakkai, who was also the subject of your first book.

Yes, but this time around I asked all sorts of critical questions. That book had only one review. Morton Smith, who had been my teacher, listed ten thousand niggling "errors," but said "nonetheless, he has proved the following fifteen important propositions."

After a couple of other books, I decided that the issue to be studied couldn't be people or topics. It had to be documents. If you're going to do anything historical, you've got to start with the bedrock. And the bedrock of the rabbinic canon is the document. That's the irreducible minimum.

When I did *Development of a Legend*, there were some critical odds and ends. A few people had made critical statements before. But these were episodic, not systematic, and were generally ignored. People in the field continued to produce the same gullible tripe they had always been writing.

What's an example of an episodic critical comment?

Well, George Foot Moore, writing on Simeon the Righteous, had said, "this material is all very legendary." But the normal procedure was like Professor Ephraim Urbach at the Hebrew University, who would say, "*yesh bazeh tziltzul shel emet*" [this has the ring of truth] or "*zeh b'vadai lo histori*" [this certainly isn't historical], and you'd want to reply, "okay, but how do you *know?*" Urbach says that if you can't prove it's not historical, you have to believe it is. I don't know why. There was no method and no reason, and there still isn't.

You have to remember that rabbinic literature was not written by trained reporters with tape recorders and TV cameras. And yet I can show you a book written as recently as one year ago in Jerusalem where the author, David Rokeach, tells you the motive of a rabbi written about in a story: "He did this because. . . ." But where are the letters, the diaries, the *evidence?*

And so Rokeach, for example, writes about these people as though there were no question that the events in question actually took place?

Right. But from the data we have, we don't really know that X really said this, or that Y really did that.

Aren't we simply talking about something as basic as the difference between science and fundamentalism?

That's my opinion. But the Israelis who work in Talmudic history would say: "Wait, we also use scientific methods." My answer to that is: "Show me. Show me where."

We'll come back to the differences between you and the Israeli scholars, but first I'd like to go back to the beginning. You were born in Hartford. . . .

In 1932. I was raised in West Hartford, where we were one of the earlier Jewish families. When I started grammar school, there were only four or five Jewish kids enrolled.

Were you aware of being Jewish?

Yes, and I'll never forget when it happened. I was in the third grade. We were drawing pictures of the Pilgrims—our New England heritage— and I assumed they were on their way to shul. I didn't want to say "shul," of course, because the teacher might not know that word. So I asked her how to spell "synagogue." And she said rather harshly: "The Pilgrims weren't *Jews*, they were *Christians*."

I was deeply offended. "They couldn't *possibly* be Christians," I told her. And I never forgave the teacher. I could never get along with her after that.

What was your Jewish life like at home?

It was typical third generation, with Yiddish-speaking grandparents and English-speaking parents. My mother learned Yiddish only after she married my father. Her mother was born in New York City, and her grandmother in Odessa. She was not a positive force for Jewishness. Just recently I took her out for supper on her 83rd birthday and she ordered scallops and ham.

But my father was very positive about being Jewish, and he was an active Zionist. For his generation Zionism was everything. He was one of the founders of the New England Zionist Region. My memories of child-hood are of being bored sitting in the car while my father went to Zion-ist meetings. He was capable of going to a different Jewish meeting every night of the week.

He also ran a Jewish newspaper, didn't he?

Oh yes, the *Connecticut Jewish Ledger*. He founded it in 1929 and ran it until 1953, when he had a stroke. My mother then ran it until 1965, when the staff bought it.

As a kid, did you have any connection with the paper?

Are you kidding? My father took it for granted that all of us would work there. In the eighth grade, in the fall, I was bar mitzvahed, and that was the end of my Jewish education, which I had genuinely enjoyed. From eighth grade through twelfth, 1945 to 1950, I had to work at the *Ledger*. So I couldn't go to Hebrew school anymore although I really wanted to.

I worked there every day after school, and often on Saturday morn-ings. There wasn't much Jewish ritual observance in our household. I didn't even know such things existed.

In high school I didn't get to participate in extracurricular clubs or activities. I was always working at the paper. I started as an errand boy. My father hired newsmen from the Hartford *Times*, and they taught me all of the editorial skills from newswriting and rewrite to layout. At the end of the school year in June, the news guys were off and I put out the paper myself for four weeks. I did it all, except that I wasn't allowed to sell advertising because I was too young.

At some point you must have resumed your Jewish education.

At the end of my junior year in high school, my parents asked me: "What do you want for your birthday?"

I asked for Hebrew lessons, which I'd never had. So every Saturday morning during my senior year I went to a teacher, Mrs. Frieda Wender, who taught me *dikduk* [grammar]. I used to bring my notebook to high school to show everybody that I was learning Hebrew. By the end of the year I had mastered the *binyanim* [Hebrew verb forms].

So you didn't exactly have a religiously Jewish upbringing.

No. Except for going to Temple, the notion of Jewish observance, even in the Reform sense, couldn't have been more alien. To me, Jewish life meant meetings and organizations and politics and announcements.

And after high school?

I went off to Harvard, and I didn't come home for the entire first year. I was afraid that if I left Harvard, it wouldn't be there when I got back. I loved it there because everybody was smart.

Is Harvard where you became interested in ancient Judaism?

Not yet. I tried everything else first. When I arrived, I went out for the fencing team, and then the soccer team. Then I decided that God wanted me to be a writer, so I took a creative writing course. I sat next to John Updike. He got an A, and I got a C. From ninth grade through college I had never had less than an A, so I decided that God wanted Updike to be a writer. I was meant for something else.

But of course you became a writer.

Well yes, of a different kind. But I couldn't do fiction.

Did the temptation to write fiction ever return to you?

No, not in the slightest. I studied American history because I knew the language. My senior thesis was on the Jews of Boston between 1880 and 1914. I was looking for my grandfather, the first Jacob Neusner. It was absolutely typical of the third generation's search for roots. My teacher was Oscar Handlin, and he didn't understand my interest. But I wanted to know who I was, and where I had come from.

What about your Jewish life at Harvard?

I used to go to services at a Reform Temple in Brookline, with Herbert Jacob, whose father was a Reform rabbi. We got on the subway every Friday night and went to Ohabei Shalom on Beacon Street. We didn't know from any other form of Jewish observance. We were genuinely pious Reform Jews.

When I was a freshman, I studied with a graduate student, Jonathan Goldstein, who's now at Iowa University. As a favor, he taught me Hebrew, the book of Ruth. He was remarkably patient and generous with me. I loved him, and I've always been grateful for the help he gave me.

Jonathan Goldstein also kept kosher, and this amazed me. I couldn't believe that anybody in the world kept kosher. Except for my grandmother, I didn't even know such people existed!

I had another friend, Henry Sosland, who also kept kosher. I couldn't understand why. He said, "I want to be a rabbi."

I said, "Well, I want to be a rabbi too, but that doesn't mean you have to keep kosher!" I had wanted to be a rabbi from the time I was thirteen. It's the only thing I ever wanted to be.

You weren't much of a shul-goer, and Jewish religious observance was the last thing on your mind. So what did being a rabbi mean to you?

It meant being very Jewish, and doing very Jewish things, whatever they might be.

Short of keeping kosher.

Right. I believed in God and all that, but who knew that Jews really *did* those things? You'd read about it in books. My grandmother was *frum*, "feathers-in-the-attic *frum*." If you keep Shabbas, you get a lot of goosefeathers and you can make a lot of pillows.

Wait a minute, I don't understand. Is that a metaphor?

No, she really believed it. She told my mother that if you keep kosher, a lot of goosefeathers will grow in your attic and you'll be able to make pillows. I guess it was part of Jewish folklore from her region in White Russia.

And after Harvard you went to the seminary?

No, first I went to Oxford. I studied with Cecil Roth, and I did a thesis on English Jews in America.

How would you evaluate Cecil Roth?

By the standards of his day, he was good. He was an antiquarian, and he knew a great deal about many things. He also did a lot of good guessing. But I don't think he had the slightest idea of what it meant to teach or how to do systematic research that had any methodological sophistication.

Now how did you, a Reform Jew, end up at the Jewish Theological Seminary ?

I was planning to go to Hebrew Union College. But Roth said, "You'll get a much better education at the Seminary." I wasn't so sure. I knew that if I went there, I'd have to start keeping kosher and everything else. But by this time I was becoming more traditional.

I was a smoker in those days, and I decided that if I could go through an entire Shabbat without smoking a cigarette, I'd apply. I was successful and the following Monday I sent off the application. I decided that if Paris was worth a mass to King Henry, then a good education was worth this *mishugaas* to me.

I went to JTS in September, and I arrived in the middle of Succot, 1954. On Shabbat, I went to services at the Seminary. I sat down next to Seymour Fox, and I asked: "What are they up to?"

"Hallel," he replied.

"Very good," I said, "What's Hallel?" I just didn't *know*. That was my initiation. As you can imagine, my first year wasn't easy. I had a little Hebrew, but I didn't know anything. Seymour Siegel was our Talmud teacher, and he was superb, a saint. He had the patience to teach us line by line. He loved the students. He was a teacher of Judaism—and by the way, of Talmud.

To keep up, I simply memorized the text. That happens to be a pretty good way to learn the Talmud, because it's such a uniform document. If you know one chapter, you know the rhetoric of fifty.

By the second year I was keeping up. We had Talmud with [Haim Zalman] Dimitrovsky and he was very good. We had Jeremiah with Shalom Spiegel, a great teacher, a truly great man. In the third year I had Shraga Abramson, another great teacher. I was like a sponge, and I had wonderful Talmud teachers throughout.

I was also Heschel's assistant. I typed the manuscript of *God in Search of Man*, which I think is his best book. Heschel was my very best influence. I survived because of him.

Survived? Wait a minute. You just told me about all these great teachers. So what was the problem?

The pressures at JTS were enormously negative. The students at that time were divided into two groups, the A's and the C's. There were some wonderfully bright people who were quite tolerant of one another, such as Yochanan Muffs, Joe Yerushalmi, Baruch Levine, David Halivni, Shmuel Leiter, Joel Kramer, Neil Gillman, Joel Zaiman, and many others. And then there was a different seminary, composed of kids who were mainly from yeshivas or from Yeshiva University. They came in order to make a living as rabbis. They couldn't stand us—and they especially couldn't stand me.

You had come from Harvard and Oxford into this parochial Jewish environment. That must have been a difficult transition.

It was, but I wasn't alone. But I got in trouble when I started to write for *Commentary*, beginning in my freshman year at JTS in 1954. This was the old *Commentary* with Elliot Cohen. I had sent them an article when I was at Oxford. They rejected the article, but they wanted me to write for them. My first article was about the founding of the Student Zionist Organization. I was also writing in many other places, including *The Reconstructionist*. All of this didn't sit too well with the Seminary.

What was the problem? Was it the chutzpah of a student publishing in Jewish magazines?

They just didn't like students who wrote. For the most part these people were not publishing scholars. And what they did publish was for other scholars. It was all very political.

As for my fellow students, the graduating class of 1955 had a class will, and they left me "a text for his commentary." Meaning: you don't know enough text, but you're busy writing in magazines. They resented it very much. I hadn't gone through the chairs they had sat in, but I was doing all of these worldly things.

How did you get involved in the Talmud?

I had found American history boring, because there was no real intellectual challenge. But when I started learning Talmud, I was just stunned by it. I found it unbelievably demanding and engaging. I was interested in the logic of people thinking clearly and rigorously, which you don't see a lot of. I was very impressed by that. I never wanted to do anything else, and I never did.

Do you still remember the first page of Talmud you ever learned?

It was Chapter 8 of Bava Qamma, about indemnity from personal injury. For me, it wasn't talking *about* Jewish anymore. It was *doing* Jewish.

Around this time you also did a doctorate at Columbia.

My last two years at JTS, 1958–60, were excruciatingly boring, so I did my Ph.D. at Columbia. JTS wasn't thrilled, but I was doing my work and I never missed a class.

I studied with Morton Smith, and my thesis was on the life of Yohanan Ben Zakkai. I received my doctorate in November of 1960, and I was asked to teach at Columbia, beginning in September of that year.

Believe me, there was no happier person on earth. I was thrilled beyond words. I had already been asked to teach at JTS, and with the chutzpah of youth, which thank God I haven't lost, I said: "I would not accept an appointment at JTS under the present administration." I really didn't think much of the ethos of the place. They were very offended, and rightly so. But I was right too.

After teaching at Columbia for one week, in September 1960, I went to the office of the acting chairman to say hello, and I said: "I'm getting my degree in another week, and I was told that when that happened I would be made an assistant professor."

He said, "Well, it so happens that I have something to tell *you*. We decided that we're not going to reappoint you next year."

After just one week?

They said they didn't want anyone in my field. But they immediately brought in David Halivni to teach my courses, so I know that wasn't the problem. I was crushed beyond words. But it got worse: Columbia University Press had given me a tentative acceptance of my book, *A Life of Yohanan*. In December 1960 my father died. I returned from sitting shivah, and in the mail was a letter from the Press informing me that they wouldn't publish my book after all. I was just crushed. It took me four years to get over it.

How do you explain these abrupt rejections?

Well, I've since learned that there's a whole tradition at Columbia of old men treating young talent badly. I think the people in charge of Jewish Studies, especially Jewish History, were not comfortable with the combination of youth, talent, ambition, and independence.

Later, Columbia did the same thing to Robert Alter and then a fellow in Hebrew literature. It's that sort of university. For me, this was a formative event. The senior people at Columbia did me in. I figured it out because I kept using them for recommendations—and then not getting the jobs or fellowships. When I stopped asking them, my luck suddenly improved. But Morton Smith stood by me in my most trying years.

The bottom line is that the old guys at Columbia and JTS hated the young guys. And I was a successful young guy, so they hated me more than other people. They made my life miserable.

Look, you know about the ones who made it, because you've heard of us. But there's a lot of people you've never heard of, not because they weren't good, but because their spirits were crushed. I still remember them, the ones who didn't survive the hatred and the envy of the old men. They were better men than I.

Are you implying that this problem is unique to Jewish academic life?

No, I think it's common in the humanities. In the hard sciences, you can replicate results, so politics and personalities play a somewhat lesser role.

At any rate, getting fired in the first week of the first year of my first job was like surviving an atomic bomb: Nothing worse can happen to you, so it's an enormously liberating experience.

What did you learn from that episode?

Not to take people too seriously, not to depend on people, and to make my own way.

Our generation had a great model not to follow: just do the opposite of our teachers, and we won't make too many mistakes. I decided to go my own way and make my own way. That was long before I had made anybody in Jerusalem or elsewhere mad at me, but it made it easy for me to deal with the Jerusalem establishment.

Let's talk about that now. What's the story?

The story is that you're not supposed to quote my work in Jerusalem. They don't review my books, they never mention them. For years my books were kept locked up, I was told. I'm an untouchable, a pariah from their perspective.

Now I don't mind if people disagree with me, but they can't pretend that I don't exist. Boycotts have nothing to do with scholarship. The Israelis boycott me; they play Arab to my Israel. It's no tribute to their scholarship, such as it is. It is a disgrace to a whole, pathetic generation of politician-scholars.

What about the young guys in Jerusalem?

The young guys are not better than the old guys. They're in a very awkward situation. The young guys can't do anything if they don't work my way, because the rest of the world laughs at them. You cannot approach the sources other than through the critical means that I've devised, and still do serious work—and everyone knows it. Everyone in Europe does it my way, and almost everyone in America, except in the usual parochial seminaries and yeshivas. But the young guys in Jerusalem cannot do it my way, so they do little, and nothing comes out anymore. As far as I know, not one book in Talmudic religion or history (except archaeology) has come out of Jerusalem in Hebrew, and certainly not in English, for the past fifteen years—nothing with new ideas.

Urbach's *Hazal [The Sage]*, published in 1969, is the last large and substantial work in Talmudic history or religion to come out of Jerusalem. Mostly they write brief, nitwit articles, or make anthologies or summarize and repeat themselves. Urbach repeats himself in his new book.

You've written somewhere that the articles in the Israeli scholarly journals *Zion* and *Tarbiz* could have been published a hundred years ago.

Absolutely.

Because?

Because they're asking the wrong questions, and their methods are all fundamentalist positivism. If the source said it happened, then it happened. But nobody works that way in ancient studies anymore. Nobody, anywhere, except the neo-Orthodox in Jerusalem, and JTSA, HUC, YU—the primitives.

Is it really that simple? If the Israeli scholars were sitting here in this room, what would they say at this point?

They wouldn't even sit here. They wouldn't give me the time of day. I've never been invited to lecture at the Hebrew University. Tel Aviv and Bar Ilan and Haifa Universities, but not Jerusalem. My books are never reviewed in Israeli journals, not one in twenty-five years.

Do you know what happened recently? Last November I was invited to give a lecture in July 1984 for the Historical Society of Israel. This is a group that's dominated by the Hebrew University crowd. You also have to understand that the phrase "historical society" has far greater import in Israel than in America. After all, over there history is nothing less than theology.

The occasion for the lecture was a celebration of the fiftieth anniversary of the journal *Zion*. I said fine, I have to be in Israel anyway, it won't even cost you any money. I gave a lot of thought to the lecture and I decided not to speak too abstractly about methodology. I made up my mind to talk about how Talmudic history was done in *Zion*.

But you evidently don't think there's much there to celebrate.

That's what I wrote in the lecture, that the articles are gullible and credulous and fundamentalist. I didn't use quite those words, but you couldn't miss my meaning. I sent it off to them in January because they wanted to translate it into Hebrew.

In March, I got a letter from a junior assistant secretary saying "we've changed our plans and we don't want foreign guests." They didn't even acknowledge that I had sent them the paper! They said "we're sorry *if* we've inconvenienced you." But I was the only one who was disinvited. Everyone else came. I don't think this sort of thing does the Israelis in this field any good. I think it's very bad for their good name.

They probably wanted a celebration of the magazine.

But what did they expect? I had never been invited to speak in Jerusalem before. It's the first invitation I ever got from them. When it was withdrawn, I wrote to them and I said: "Okay, you've shown me who you are and what you are." It was very liberating.

Does the rest of the world take their work seriously?

It's not a question of who takes whose work seriously. That's mere politics. Their "work" isn't coming out. You've read *The Structure of Scientific Revolution?* Kuhn talks about changes in paradigms. When the evidence is different, the questions shift completely. One of the things that make s a difference is *who does work.* In Israel they do a lot of articles about *pintelach*, little points about this and that.

Such as?

Such as what time in the morning Pontius Pilate went to the toilet. Or whose skull did Hillel see floating on the water? Or the day that Rav Shilah hit somebody on the head with a bucket. Or the conception of X in the book of Y. They're at the stage of hunting and gathering, of what we in America call "show and tell." In the Talmud area, all they're doing is collecting and arranging variant readings, and working on enormously erudite philology that doesn't make much difference to the meaning of the text. There's no critical program, no method and no system. Someone at Bar Ilan gives a seminar on locks and keys in Talmudic literature. They've come to that—sad but silly.

Now when I talk this way about Israeli scholars, I mean in this one field, in Talmudic and related historical studies. Israelis do other things very well, but that doesn't do me any good. I have an enormous audience in Israel outside of my immediate area, especially in Bible and History. My recent book, *Judaism: The Evidence of the Mishnah*, is being translated into Hebrew.

But if you went to a lecture in Israel and you raised your hand and asked: "How do we know if Rav Shimon really said that?" they ask "*Atah talmido shel Noise-nur?*" [Are you a student of Neusner?]. In a way, it's a great honor. They've given me credit for everything that's happened in the Western Humanities since the Enlightenment!

Why doesn't this same kind of conflict arise in biblical scholarship?

Because there you don't have to deal with the modern Orthodox. They reject Biblical scholarship out of hand. It doesn't interest them, and they're afraid of it. But in fact it is a problem in that area too. They're still upset about the discovery of Third Isaiah—a hundred years ago!

But the Talmud they think they own. That's what makes them *them*. I've invaded the sacred preserve, and what's more, I treat it as totally secular. And by translating this stuff, I also ruin its mystery. They can no longer ladle out, secret by secret, the way [Saul] Lieberman did, this source and that source. Now, anyone who wants to look can look. And it's true. If you don't like my translation of the Palestinian Talmud, then improve on it. I'll be the first one to applaud. But it's no longer a secret.

There's another dimension to the problem. We in the Diaspora are not supposed to *be* Jewish scholars. We're supposed to be singing Christmas carols on our way to the gas chambers with our goyishe wives. It's bad enough that I work in a Jewish area . But I also work in the holy area, and I publish a lot. And outside of Israel I'm the dominant figure in this field.

Do you still send students to Jerusalem?

Sure, all the time. But they don't say they're my students. That's nobody's business. They're there to learn, and we tell them, "don't say who you are or what you think about anything. Just learn what there is to be learned, and then come home. Don't ask questions." We're Marranos.

And what exactly do they learn there?

The Israelis do a very good job of language and text teaching. You've got to have people to sit in a classroom and explain what the text means. But you've also got to be careful, because if you raise your hand and ask "How do we know that Rabbi Akiva really said that?" they say, "Oh, you're from Brown!"

Wait a minute. On the one hand you talk about having an enormous influence. But at the same time you complain that you're not getting a fair hearing.

It's a paradox. I have an enormous hearing in the scholarly world, in religious studies and the humanities. My scholarly books sell very well. Outside of Israel, everyone in the academic study of religion knows my work, absorbs it, uses it, and it's a perfectly normal professional transaction. There are not many distinguished universities where I haven't lectured. That's why the Israelis and the parochial types in this country say, "He writes for the goyim." They treated Buber and Heschel even worse. I'm proud to talk about Judaism to all whom it may concern.

The other side is that I've never been invited to lecture at a Rabbinical school in this country or abroad.

Not even HUC?

Not HUC in Cincinnati or in New York. I'm invited to meals in private homes, but not to the campus.

Not the Reconstructionists?

I lectured there in their first year, when the place was a disaster. I don't even put that on my resume. I did once give a summer course at JTS, but that didn't work well. After that I became a pariah there, and I haven't been there since. Only one Jewish institution in this country has received me in any way. That's Dropsie, but it's a perfectly secular place.

There *is* a paradox here. The worldly acceptance has been enormous. But on the other side, there is the other world, Jerusalem and the U.S. Jewish seminaries and yeshivas which are very hostile and which don't want to argue with me. I can't blame them.

Do you think that part of this is an antagonism to somebody who's very prolific?

I don't think that would matter, *if* I were saying things that they wanted to hear. I don't detect any antagonism toward Salo Baron, who is prolific, because he doesn't upset anybody. He just collects a lot of information. Why get mad at him?

But you do publish an enormous amount, and people tend to focus on that. The other day somebody said to me, "The problem with Jack is that he writes faster than most people can read." And somebody else, when he heard I was coming to interview you, said: "Ask him how he does it! Does he really use two typewriters at once, one for each hand?" I always think of you in terms of the novelist Joyce Carol Oates, who would probably have a better literary reputation if she published less often. Do you think you're punished for publishing too much?

Perhaps. But you *can* read one book at a time and listen to one message at a time. I've long ago decided that I'm going to do things my way. I just have more ideas than a lot of people.

And more energy.

I guess so.

How *do* you publish so much? Do you write all the time?

No. To me a good working day is three to four hours. I'm in my study by 7:30 or 8 in the morning, and I work until around 10:30 or 11. Then I swim a half-mile, have lunch with colleagues, meet students, give classes—the usual. I also work another hour or two after supper. One reason I'm fast is that I write in my head before putting things on paper. I'll work on an essay for months in my head. When I go to write it, I just put it down on paper as fast as I can type.

When I was working on Mishnah, tractate Ohalot, for example, I was deeply puzzled by the intractability of the central thesis of the tractate. I had memorized the bulk of it and kept repeating the main points

to myself. Driving down Hope Street in Providence, I had the bright
idea of reversing the predicate and the subject of some of the principal
propositions of the tractate. All of a sudden everything fell into place. I
was so stunned I almost drove into a tree.

Do you think you're prolific in part because you're controversial?

No, I don't live on other peoples' energy. Only on my own. Well, I
once asked Richard Rubenstein how to respond to a particularly virulent
and irrational review by Solomon Zeitlin. He said to me, "Write another
book. The issue is murder, so you affirm life." My whole career has been
an affirmation of life. I don't mean in the abstract, but minute by minute. I used to fear dying young, before I got anything done. I was so
glad to pass thirty, then thirty-six—Mozart was my hero. Then forty,
now fifty-two. My God, fifty-two. What a gift!

**Let's get more concrete. How are you so productive, and what ad-
vice can you give to those of us who want to increase our productivity?**

I work hard. I treasure the minutes, but I'm also one of the great
batlanim [time-wasters] of the age. As far as I know, I spend more time
with my undergraduates than any other professor at Brown, and I love
the time I spend with most of them. I also spend more time with my
graduate students than anyone else in graduate education anywhere. Of
that I am sure. And I always have time for my colleagues. I spend time,
you should pardon me, gossiping on the phone with people I adore, near
and far, getting their views on every sort of subject. I can be a real pest.

"Productivity" isn't quantitative. It can mean one book or a hundred.
Franck wrote one symphony, Brahms wrote only four symphonies,
whereas Mozart composed ten times that number, and Haydn still more.
Who is to say who was the greatest composer of the lot? Each person
does what he or she does. God endows us all, and we are judged—and
we judge ourselves—only by how we use God's gifts.

Should I hate Robert Redford because he is handsomer than I am? I
have colleagues at least as smart and as hard-working as I am, and they
create in media other than books. Why make comparisons?

The main thing in writing a lot of books is having a lot of things you
want to say in books. If you have nothing to say in a book, you won't
write a book. If you have a lot to say, and if, in addition, you have the
capacity and the courage to sit down and write it, then you'll publish.
You'll also make a lot of enemies.

Productivity breeds contempt?

I once asked Gershom Scholem when the hatred stops. He replied:
"When I turned forty, they got used to me."

I asked Harry Wolfson, who had been my freshman adviser at Harvard, a man of remarkably honorable character, when "it" would end.
He said to me, "If you want people to like you, stop writing, stop publishing, stop saying new things. Above all, stop criticizing the work of

other people. Then everyone will love you. But if you don't, just go on doing what you're doing, and they'll get used to you."

I don't think that's how things have worked out so far, but I don't really mind, one way or the other. I don't work to spite anyone, or to impress anyone either, but only to please myself and to say what is welling up and demands to be said.

How many books have you published?

If you count each volume, including children's books, anthologies, and everything else, it's, probably around two hundred. Maybe more, counting revisions, translations into various languages, and new editions.

And how many more are in press?

Another fifty or so. But that's including each of the tractates of the Yerushalmi and Bavli translations. Still, it's a lot.

While we're on the subject of publications, I'd like to get your view of a few Jewish newspapers and magazines.

Sure.

Let's start with *Commentary*.

They're pathetic, bitter enemies of Judaism. They stopped pretending to be Jewish in 1960, when Norman [Podhoretz] took over. He took out the mezuzzahs on the doors, the Cedars of Lebanon column and other things. He didn't even want to pretend to be Jewish.

A few years later he did his political shift, which I happen to respect and share, but he never did a shift on anything Jewish. The magazine doesn't even pretend that Judaism is a living religion, that Jewish intellectual life has substance and discipline and method and important issues to debate. It in no way takes seriously that the Jews are Jewish *in their minds*. That's why *Commentary* is the most destructive Jewish institution around. It tells people every month that there's nothing important about the Jewish intellect.

That doesn't mean they don't sometimes publish a good article on a Jewish theme. Robert Alter and Jacob Katz are consistently very good. But this is clearly *pro forma*. And by treating it as such with so little else of a Jewish intellectual character of such high quality, they underline the message, which is that the action is somewhere else. And yet they are Jewish. And yet it's the American *Jewish* Committee. And yet they want a Jewish audience. It's enormously destructive.

And *Judaism*?

It's dead. [Robert] Gordis killed it. He took a magazine where people could argue about important issues, and he turned it into an intellectual embarrassment, a self-celebration of third-rate minds. It's not even boring! It's just show and tell, "X's view of Y." Here too there are occasional good articles, but only by accident. It didn't have to be that way. Steven [Schwarzschild], a great man, a moral hero, never should have resigned. Had he known what would happen to the magazine, he wouldn't have left.

It's a great loss, and now we don't have a serious intellectual journal. *Midstream* prints slander to get attention. *Conservative Judaism* is a filthy rag. The *Jewish Spectator* is the closest thing to a worthy journal of opinion, but it's not well supported. We'll see if *New Traditions* can fill the bill. Curiously, *Response* never died. It's odd, it's uneven , but it's always retained the ability to be interesting. I love to print my work there, and also in the reborn *Reconstructionist*. There's a whole new generation.

Ten years ago, when I gave up the editorship of *Response*, you advised me to kill the magazine.

I was wrong. I didn't think it would retain consistent vitality and standing. But it has, and it's still interesting. *Response* ran a terrific piece not long ago by Ivan Marcus. It was called "This Year in Jerusalem," and it was a devastating description of academic politics in Israel.

Response is kind of a cult. It's whoever is in the office that day. It's Our Crowd. But they're open, and they're a good crowd. They're not a coterie journal like *Prooftexts*. *They* really are the narcissists. They publish the same nine people in every issue—and *nobody* else. Nobody exists if they're not part of their crowd. That's something that we at Brown have been accused of, by the way, but that's not true of us. We invite everybody to our conferences. We print everyone in our series. But these people organize a journal and they publish just themselves.

That's my problem with *Prooftexts*. They don't care if anybody even understands them, so long as they can show off in their long, recondite articles. Welcome to hard-core *Wissenchaft des Judentums*, as practiced by the younger generation.

And *Modern Judaism*?

I think the magazine has no voice because it covers everything: literature, history, politics, sociology—everything and its opposite. The real problem is that there's no field theory that draws together all the data for modern Judaism.

They too have published some good articles. But there have also been some terrible ones, and overall the magazine is not yet even mediocre. There's no taste, no judgment—just politics, the editor's friends. I recently read Steve Katz's article about the "uniqueness" of the Holocaust. I think it's intellectually vulgar. It comes down to why the Shoah was "worse" than what the Armenians went through. Now why would anyone want to talk about that?

Are you kidding? People want to talk about that all the time. It's the Olympics of suffering.

It's true. A group of Holocaust survivors right here in Providence held a meeting where they debated which concentration camp was worse: "You didn't go through anything compared to what I went through." I can't think of anything more grotesque.

I think it's equally grotesque for us to be arguing with other ethnic groups that our Holocaust was worse than their Holocaust. Is our blood redder than theirs? It's not a discussion that pays tribute to the human greatness of the Jewish people, to our dignity, or to our sense of self-worth. If you know who you are, you don't have to make statements like that. You don't found the consciousness of who you are on the fact that you've got cancer—or survived cancer. I don't see anything positive in that formulation.

But let's get back to magazines. You didn't ask me about *Moment*.

No?

I don't think Leibel [Leonard Fein] ever decided what he wanted to do with it. And you can't write for him but have him rewrite your article to be *his* article. That's why I quit.

He sometimes rewrites pretty extensively. But I haven't minded because my articles always get better in the process.

Mine too, but not always. He's a good editor, but I got tired of *sounding* like him. But that's not the real problem. There's no Torah in *Moment*, there's no content. It's all politics and Jewish nostalgia.

For my money, Fein's political articles are the best around.

True, but the nostalgia—the Jewish message—is repetitious and tedious and very subjective. And the Jewish stuff that he does print rarely has depth. For example, I've begged him to include book reviews.

That's not only *Moment*'s problem. There's no serious book reviewing in any of the Jewish periodicals.

I know it first-hand. My books are virtually never reviewed in Jewish publications.

Over the years, I've toyed with the idea of starting a Jewish Review of Books.

Well, there's *Judaica Book News*.

But it's pretty quirky.

True, but it's honest and decent. Brown uses it for library orders.

Do you like any of the newspapers? I see that you get the *Baltimore Jewish Times*. I think that's about the only good one around.

Well, I prefer the Washington paper. It's a real paper, and it's fun to read. And the Philadelphia paper is very good. It's enormous. I also like the Long Island **Jewish World**, the *Advocate* in Boston, and the Denver paper.

I agree with you about Long Island and I've heard good things about Washington. I've never seen the Denver paper, but for my money, the Jewish papers in Philadelphia and Boston are vastly over-rated. But let's move on and talk a little about the Jewish community. You've complained about this recent obsession with the Holocaust.

It's not so recent. I've been complaining about it since 1969. Then in 1971 Michael Wyschogrod said it better than I did with a review of

Fackenheim's book in *Judaism*. But I was wrong: I thought the thing would peter out. Instead, it's still going.

Arthur Hertzberg has said that the Holocaust is a very easy, accessible Jewish experience, a "cheap thrill." He's right. It will always produce an audience. It will always produce a visible, guaranteed reaction. It's exploitation.

I share your concern. There are many people for whom learning about the Holocaust seems to be their primary Jewish experience.

It won't last. Why would you want to be Jewish just so you can suffer?

What else disturbs you about contemporary Jewish life?

That's easy: the absence of *Ahavat Yisrael*, which I would translate as "love for oneself as a Jew and for one's fellow Jews." Everybody has to be special, and nobody wants to respect anyone else. There's a lot of arrogance toward other Jews. The Orthodox are parading around, saying: "We're going to make it. When there's only three quarters of a million Jews left in America, we'll be them." I think this is pathetic, and also very dangerous. They believe their own press notices as they write them. The other sects are no more generous in spirit, either.

In general, the Jewish community doesn't want to talk to other people. We've always got to be superior, always have to feel persecuted. Otherwise, we can't be Jewish. I think this attitude is disgraceful.

While we're on the topic of the Jewish community, I want to mention the havurah phenomenon. Long before there was a "havurah movement," you were writing on this topic. What got you interested in it?

In the late 1950s I had been working on the concept of the *haver* and the *havurah* in the Mishnah. I compared the *havurah* to the *yahad*, that is, the community formed by the Jews at the Dead Sea, known to us from the Dead Sea scrolls. I began thinking about the basic principles of social organization of religion that were represented by the early havurot, and they seemed to me to solve certain basic problems facing the synagogues and the temples that I knew. So I wrote a few articles and made a number of speeches on the subject. These led to two books: *Fellowship in Judaism, the First Century and Today*, published by Vallentine Mitchell back in 1963, and an anthology called *Contemporary Judaic Fellowship in Theory and in Practice*, published by Ktav in 1972.

I know that book well because I wrote a long piece for you about havurat shalom. You also included articles by Alan Mintz, Art Green, Everett Gendler and Zalman Schachter, if I'm not mistaken. Every now and then somebody comes to interview me about the contemporary havurah phenomenon, and I always tell them to start by reading that book. In most cases they already have.

You know, people don't really grasp that the things they do, practical things, begin in ideas, commitments, concerns, even yearning. That is to say, practical action begins in reflection, and ideas do matter. Everything we do was thought up by someone, whether it's a Jewish state, which was thought up in a book, or living an ethical life, which was also thought up in a book. The idea of the havurot as a renewed form of Judaic social organization began somewhere. And, in fact, it was in my head.

To move to the larger Jewish community, do you see any bright spots in contemporary Jewish life?

Sure, lots of them. I'm basically an optimistic person. The main one is obvious: the fourth generation. There wasn't supposed to be one. We in America know something that Jews haven't yet learned in other parts of the Diaspora—how to transmit "being Jewish" to free people who have choices. I'm not sure the Israelis have done as well.

Do you mean it's working?

We *know* it's working. By teaching, I'm always fifteen years ahead of the Jewish community. As a result, I get a preview of the next generation before the Jewish community sees them. In my classes I'm seeing kids whose *great* grandparents spoke English without an accent. These kids want to be Jewish, and they're very serious about it, and there are lots of them. That's something we had no reason to expect.

But you can't speak to these people as though they're European, or as though they're inferior, or afraid, or coerced, or as though if you don't tell them every fifteen minutes that they're special, that they're the best, and that the world hates them, they'll stop being Jewish. You have to treat them as if being Jewish is normal to their lives, or you won't have anything to say to them. Because it's now perfectly normal to be Jewish in America.

Look: there's a boy in my class who's on the university swim team. He's the most outdoor person you'll ever meet. He spends the summer climbing rocks in Colorado. He's blond and blue-eyed. He's polite and sweet-natured and he's a first-rate student. But he didn't go to Duke because he thought it was anti-Semitic.

I said, "Gee, David , you could have passed!" He looked at me like I was crazy. He didn't have the slightest idea of what I meant. That's a bright spot—one among many.

We in the universities are talking to the Jews as they really are. I don't think the rest of the Jewish world is. They're only interested in the kind of Jews they *want* to see. But we don't have a choice. We see them all as students.

The tragedy is the rabbinate. They just didn't keep up, and now they've become irrelevant. Their training is irrelevant, their message is irrelevant, their institutions are irrelevant. It didn't have to be that way.

Who *is* keeping up?

I think the Federations are. I think they're worthwhile. They have a bottom line, and they're very professional about it. Outside of the Federations, there's a deep anti-professionalism in the Jewish community. People make things up as they go along . . .

And they call it Judaism.

Exactly. They're happy, and they don't want to be bothered. The Federations, by contrast, have a job to do. There's policy, there's reflectiveness, and there's effectiveness. You may not think that raising money is the whole point, but at least somebody is doing something.

Unfortunately, there's still a lot of slovenliness and Jewish self-hatred in the Jewish community. Like coming late to programs, or not making the effort to do something well. But there are plenty of exceptions, and a lot of people who have a sense of honor and commitment.

More bright spots?

Among the organizations, Hadassah. As for individuals, Carmi Schwartz and Darrell Friedman from the Council of Jewish Federations and Welfare Funds. Trude Weiss-Rosmarin, editor of the *Jewish Spectator*. And Yitz [Irving] Greenberg is truly good. He spoke recently in Providence about the Holocaust, and did a first-rate job. Everybody respected him, including the faculty. It was a talk that wouldn't embarrass you, a talk that was definitely not exploitative. Greenberg has a lot of Jewish dignity. He's a fine man and a great Jew.

And he's not alone: there are a lot of fine men and women around. And by the way, I've noticed something interesting, and this is another bright spot. The good people know and respect each other.

We're out of time. But before we stop, is there anything that I should have asked you but didn't? Anything that you'd like to add?

Only that it's much more worthwhile being Jewish than a lot of people realize. As Heschel used to say, the human materials of the Jewish community are undervalued and underappreciated. We have a great supply of good people. I see their children all the time. They have true Jewish loyalty and commitment, and curiosity as well. Their parents deserve some credit, too, for making these kids into hopeful Jews. That's why, despite some disappointments, I'm optimistic about our future.

INDEX

Abramson, Shraga, 119
Ahavat Israel, 130
Alter, Robert, 121, 127
American Academy of Religion, 18
Aqiva, martyrdom of, 96–100
Assimilation and Jewish learning,
    29–31, 33–34

Baltimore Jewish Times, 129
Bar Ilan University, 122–23
Baron, Salo, 125
Bellah, Robert, 19
Bennett, William, 43–44
Bland, Kalman P., 39
Brilling, Bernhard, 73
Brandeis University, 11, 40–41, 49
Buber, Martin, 125

Cohen, Elliot, 62, 119
Cohen, Gerson D., 30
Columbia University, 40
Columbia University Press, 120
Commentary, 119, 127
Connecticut Jewish Ledger, 116
Conservative Judaism, 128
Conservative Judaism and freedom of
    thought in Judaic studies, 71–84

Dimitrovsky, Haim Zalman, 119
Douglas, 19, 110
Dropsie University, 125
Duke University, 39–40, 50
Durkheim, E., 16, 19, 110

Eliberg-Schwartz, Howard, 39
Eliezer ben Hyrcanus, 106
Enlightenment and Jewish-Judaic
    studies, 6–7

Fackenheim, E., 130
Fasman, Oscar, 61, 64
Fein, Leonard, 129
Fernandez, James, 110
Fox, Seymour, 118
Frankel, Zechariah, 72–76
Freedom of thought in Jewish and
    Judaic studies, 61–69, 71–84

Freud, Sigmund, 16
Friedman, Darrell, 132

Geertz, C., 19
Gendler, Everett, 130
Gereboff, Joel, 73
Gillman, Neil, 119
Ginzberg, Louis, 64, 66
Goldstein, Jonathan, 117
Gordis, Robert, 127
Green, Arthur, 87–88, 130
Green, William Scott, 3
Greenberg, Irving, 132

Haifa University, 122
Halivni, David, 119–20
Handlin, Oscar, 117
Hartford (CT) *Times*, 116
Harvard University, 40
Hebrew Union College, 65, 118, 122,
    125
Hertzberg, Arthur, 130
Herzl, Theodor, 27
Heschel, A. J., 125, 132
Hirsch, Samson Raphael, 73, 80
Historical Society of Israel, 122
Humanities, interaction of disciplines
    of religious studies, 15–21
Hurwitz, Henry, 62

Indiana University, 40
Israel, State of, universities and Jewish
    learning, 27–37

Jacob, Herbert, 117
Jewish Advocate (Boston), 129–30
Jewish and Judaic studies, 6, 85–100;
    continuity in studies, 96–99;
    creation of university studies,
    39–50; criticism in disciplines for,
    61–69; enlightenment, 6–7,
    freedom of thought in studies,
    61–69, 71–84; methodology in
    studies, 109–12; objectives in,
    11–25, 86–90, 100; professional
    standards for, 51–57, 61–69;
    sectarian influences in, 61–69,
    86–90, 114; as social science, 40;

Talmudic studies, phases of, 103–8; universities and Jewish learning, 27–37
Jewish Spectator, 128
Jewish Theological Seminary of America, 65, 103, 118–22, 125; at Breslau, 72–73
Judaism, 127, 130

Katz, Jacob, 127
Katz, Steve, 128
Klein, Shelomo, 73, 80
Kramer, Joel, 119
Kuhn, Thomas, 123

Language, foreign language in religious studies, 20–22, 24–25
Leach, Edmund, 110
Leiter, Shmuel, 119
Levine, Baruch, 119
Lieberman, Saul, 124
Long Island *Jewish World*, 129–30
Luther, Martin, 67

Maimonides, 80–81
Marcus, Ivan, 128
Merton, Robert K., 62–65, 68
Meyers, Eric M., 39
Midstream, 128
Mintz, Alan, 130
Modern Judaism, 128
Moment, 129
Moore, George Foot, 115
Muffs, Yochanan, 119

National Council on the Humanities, 25
National Endowment for the Humanities, 25, 43
New Traditions, 128
Nordau, Max Simon, 27

Oates, Joyce Carol, 125
Ohio State University, 40

Perry, Edward, 110
Podhoretz, Norman, 127
Prooftexts, 128
Protestant culture and religious studies in contemporary world, 18

Rappoport, Shelomo, 73
The Reconstructionist, 119, 128
Reform Judaism, freedom of thought in Judaic studies, 71–84; university study and Jewish learning, 27–37
Religious studies and community life, 110; in contemporary world, 14–17; discovery of self, 22–24, foreign languages for study, 20–22, 24–25; humanities and interaction of disciplines, 15–21; methodology, 109–12; protestant culture and contemporary world, 18
Response, 128
Ritterband, Paul, 28
Rokeach, David, 115
Roth, Cecil, 118
Rubenstein, Richard, 126

Sarton, George, 62
Schachter, Zalman, 130
Schiffman, Lawrence H., 82
Scholarship and freedom for discourse, 4–9
Schwartz, Carmi, 132
Schwarzchild, Steven, 128
Self, discovery of in religious studies, 22–24
Sholem, Gershom, 127
Siegel, Seymour, 119
Simeon the Righteous, 115
Sklare, Marshall, 28–29, 33–34
Smart Foundation, 39–40, 50
Smith, Jonathan Z., 47–48, 96
Smith, Morton, 114, 120–21
Sosland, Henry, 118
Spiegel, Shalom, 119
Student Zionist Organization, 119

Talmudic studies, 120; phases of, 103–8
Tarbiz, 122
Tel Aviv University, 122
Thackray, Arnold, 62–65, 68
Torah, Oral Torah and Mishnah in Judaic studies, 72–73
Turner, Victor, 110

University of Minnesota, 40
University of North Carolina, 40
University of Wisconsin, 40
Updike, John, 117
Urbach, Ephraim, 115, 122

Weber, Ernst Heinrich, 16, 110
Weis-Rosmarin, Trude, 132
Weizman, Chaim, 27
Wender, Frieda, 117
Weschsler, Harold, 62